# A Level Study Guide: Euripides' *Medea*

*Athena Critical Guides*

## Introduction

### A Level Study Guide: Euripides' *Medea*

This study guide has been written to assist the learner in understanding the play and context of Euripides' *Medea*.

This Study Guide will assist in understanding and examining Euripides' *Medea* in the wider context of Greek tragedy and the Athenian society in which it was produced and first performed.

Euripides' *Medea* is a popular text for students of Ancient Greek Civilization, but is also a popular text for students of Theatre Studies and is also of interest as a pathway text for learners undertaking additional credit courses such as the Extended Project and remains a common choice for those working towards the International Baccalaureate.

This study guide is also suitable for those interested in Greek Tragedy for the enjoyment of the plays themselves. After all, Greek Tragedy is one of the world's great achievements and within the stories and myths of the Greek Tragedies are the origins of many of the great literary works which were produced and an influence for plays and stories being written today.

### Who is this study guide for?

This study guide is intended to offer a satisfying experience for those learners who undertake an **AS or A level qualification in Classical Civilization**.

This qualification is offered by CIE and OCR examination boards and this resource is primarily designed to assist those who are studying for this qualification.

However this Study Guide will also help to lay a sound foundation for those who go on to study the Ancient World at a higher (degree) level as well as appeal to those who are interested in learning more about the ancient world.

**Please note that this study guide is not endorsed by CIE or OCR and as such is not an officially recognized product by CIE or OCR.**

This Study Guide is however designed to be used as a study aide in order to help learners to attain a qualification in the following examination unis;

- CIE: Classical Studies 9274: Paper 4 Classical Literature: Sources and Evidence Drama: the idea of tragedy

- OCR: Classical Civilisation: Paper 2: The Invention of the Barbarian (H408/23)

**About Athena Online Education**

Athena Online Education comprises of a specialist team of professional course writers based in the UK, Greece and Spain. All course writers are highly-qualified subject specialists and are experienced teachers, lecturers and course writers, as well as being experienced and current examination assessors for the main examination boards, including CIE, AQA, OCR and Edexcel.

**About the Author**

Paul Kenney is an experienced course writer, college lecturer and tutor, and examiner for several examination boards. A graduate of the University of Wales and postgraduate of Nottingham University in Classics and Archaeology, he has been examining, tutoring and writing courses and course materials since 2005.

**IMPORTANT PLEASE READ!**

**Candidates taking the CIE A Level Classical Studies**

The CIE in Classical Studies 9274 Paper 4 is an A level unit and comprises the study of 4 plays, as well as the context in which they were produced and performed.

These plays are;

- Aeschylus *Agamemnon*
- Sophocles *Oedipus Tyrannus*
- Euripides *Medea*
- Seneca *Oedipus*

**Candidates taking the OCR A Level in Classical Civilisation**

The Invention of the Barbarian (H408/23) Paper 2 is an A level unit and comprises the study of two plays and one History text;

- Aeschylus' *Persians*
- Euripides' *Medea*
- Herodotus' *The Histories*

### Translations of Euripides' *Medea*

Both CIE and OCR Examination boards do not recommend any set translation of Euripides' *Medea*.

*Any translation is valid and may be used by a learner.*

However, the following translations are commonly available;

Euripides' *Medea* - translated by P Vellacott (Penguin)

Free versions of the play can be obtained from;

The Perseus digital Library;

www.perseus.tufts.net

Both Kindle and iBooks also may offer free or purchasable versions of Euripides' *Medea* which may be used accompany this study guide.

**Studying tragic plays** – when studying Greek Tragedy at A level, it is recommended that you consider the following bullet points as you progress through the plays;

- Consider how the narratives and techniques of Euripides differ from those of Sophocles and Aeschylus? For example, how do the chorus and actors convey information or display emotion?

- How does the tragedian present themes and issues such as women/society/gods/ justice and revenge/ war and morality?

- Consider the choice of language used in the play. How effectively has the tragedian employed language and dialects used by both the chorus and actors? For example, do the characters speak formally or informally? Why do you think that the author elected to use the language they do?

### Aeschylus, Sophocles and Euripides: The Greek Tragedians

Throughout the 5$^{th}$ century BC hundreds of tragedies were written and performed across the cities of Greece and by many different playwrights.

However, the only complete plays that survive were written by three tragedians: Aeschylus, Sophocles and Euripides. All of these authors were Athenian and although their plays were later reproduced in many theatres across the Greek world, they were all produced initially for an Athenian audience in the city of Athens.

Aeschylus is the earliest surviving playwright. He wrote over seventy plays, of which seven survive today.

Sophocles is thought to have written one hundred and twenty three plays, of which seven also survive.

Euripides is thought to have written ninety two plays, and of these, some nineteen survive. It is apparent then that the majority of plays have been lost entirely, or are available only in fragmentary form, preserved by other writers from the Greek and Roman period as quotations.

The lives of these three tragedians covered just over a hundred years, though their careers overlapped each other. Aeschylus was born in the 520s BC and died in 456 BC. Sophocles was born in the 490s BC and died in 406 BC. Euripides was born in the 480s BC and died just shortly before Sophocles in 407/6BC. The careers of these three great writers cover the fifth century BC, a period which saw the flourishing of tragedy as an art form, as well as the rise and fall of the Athenian Empire.

**Euripides**

Euripides was born in Athens around 484BC and first competed in the *City Dionysia* festival in 455BC and died around 407/6BC, not in Athens, but in the kingdom of Macedonia.

Euripides was a prolific writer, writing at least ninety plays, of which nineteen have survived and nine of these are datable;

*Alcestis (438), Medea (431), Hippolytus (428), Andromache, Hecuba, Trojan Women (415), Helen (412), Phoenician Women (409), Orestes (408), Bacchae (408-406), Rhesus, Electra, Heraclids, Heracles, Suppliant Women, Iphigenia at Aulis (408-406), Iphigenia among the Taurians, Ion and Cyclops.*

According to some hostile and later commentators, relative lack of success at Athens prompted Euripides to leave his home city and travel to Macedonia at the invitation of the Macedonian King and it was in Macedon that he died.

Euripides died having written several still unperformed plays. He won a posthumous victory for his *Bacchae*. Euripides won the *City Dionysia* competition four times and in this sense was the least successful of the three Tragedians whose plays survive. Despite this, his plays resonate with modern audiences and are among the most popular today.

**Euripides' formal introduction and conclusion of plays**

Euripides' plays typically commence with a prologue which consists of a monologue by one of the protagonists in the play. In the *Medea*, the monologue is performed by the Nurse. The Nurse is a household slave of Medea and Jason (Medea's husband) and the Nurse introduces the play and supplies the audience with details of events leading up to the conclusion that they are about to witness.

Euripides typically (although not always) concludes his plays with an intervention from the immortal gods. In the *Medea*, Euripides diverges from this structure slightly.

The end of the play is very dramatic and striking. Medea is mounted aboard a chariot drawn by dragons that her Grandfather the Sun God has provided. In this chariot Medea will depart Corinth as a vengeful Goddess, taking the bodies of her slaughtered children with her and leaving Jason broken and distraught, denied even the comfort of their burial.

### The Role of Women in Euripides' plays

Euripides departs from the other surviving tragedians in that he often portrays women as avengers as well as victims. This is well illustrated in *Medea*; as the eponymous heroine is both the wronged victim and also intent on deadly revenge. In this play Euripides portrays Medea as a bitter and manipulative woman, who presents herself in part as a helpless victim to Creon and Jason in turn, but all the while Medea is intent on her revenge for the wrongs that have been inflicted upon her.

The tragedy of *Medea* begins with Medea offstage, cursing and screaming her grief at the news that she has been abandoned by Jason, yet by the end of the play Medea has been transformed into a flying sorceress, who has defeated and outwitted all of her adversaries through her powerful speeches and deceptive actions, and inflicted murder on the innocent children as well as those against whom she had grievance. However, the main target of her ire, Jason, is spared. It is more cruel to leave him alone and alive.

### Euripides' realism

According to Aristotle the Greek tragedian Sophocles portrayed people as they **ought** to be, whereas Euripides portrays people as they actually **are**.

For example, Creon in the *Medea* comes across as both decisive and determined when he enters stage, but ends up manipulated and uncertain. He leaves the stage knowing he has made the wrong decision in allowing Medea to remain for an additional day in Corinth, but vacillates between his duty to protect his own family from a known villain, and pity for Medea and Jason's children.

Medea, on the other hand, is a more complex character, who undergoes a transformation on stage as the play progresses; from an angry and enraged woman to a divine force above the laws of men.

Medea may undergo a transformation, but her desire to wreak vengeance on the one hand, and her love for the children that she must kill on the other, are a credit to Euripides' awareness of depth of character and the conflict within her that she must resolve as part of her transformation.

**Euripides the innovator**

According to Aristophanes, Euripides was an innovative play writer who liked to add new components to his plays. For example, in the *Medea*, the children are present on stage for much of the action, but are silent. The Princess Glauce however is utterly absent from the stage, but her death is retold vividly through the speech of the Messenger.

Euripides also attempts in *Medea* to limit the importance and role of the chorus. One modern commentator refers to the role of the Chorus in *Medea* as 'embarrassing'. There are apparent grounds for this criticism. The Chorus does little in this play.

This deliberate decision by Euripides to limit the role and importance of the Chorus has been characterized as an attempt to make his plays more entertaining to the audience, by strengthening the importance of the actors, but perhaps this was the reason why the play failed to win the *City Dionysia*.

## PART ONE: An Introduction to Greek Tragedy:

## Key concepts

## 1.1 An introduction to Greek Tragedy

This section will help you to;

- *Explore the difference between the ancient Greek and modern theatre.*

- *Identify what a Greek Theatre looked like and consider some of its components.*

- *Consider the nature of dramatic festivals and competitions in 5th century Athens.*

- *Explain the deployment and use of some of the stage machinery and theatre buildings.*

**Comparing the ancient and modern theatre**

Despite having its roots in the Ancient Greek theatre, modern theatre is very different. First of all, modern theatre is primarily for entertainment. In contrast, Ancient Athenian theatre productions, although they were entertaining and engaging for the audience, were an integral part of Athenian religious festivals that were designed to unite the Athenian citizen body as well as honouring the gods of the *polis* (city).

Modern-day theatre audiences tend to be largely directed towards the middle classes of society, with the majority of audiences being comprised of adults. However the range of theatre on offer can and does have the capability of attracting a broad spectrum of people of all ages and from all sections of society. In 5th century Athens, the audience was primarily if not entirely male and comprised a good proportion of the citizen body. Whether women did or did not attend the theatre is still debated.

Another difference between the ancient and modern theatre is that the modern audience would only expect to see one play at a time. In Athens at the festivals where they were performed the audience would watch several plays in a row; all by the same author and often interconnected. Perhaps the closest modern comparison would be to view a trilogy of films in succession such as the *Star Wars* trilogy.

A modern audience also expect and choose to go to the theatre at any time during the year. In London's West End, for example, there are a wide range of plays performed daily; some of which have been performed day on day for years. A typical ancient Athenian citizen would only see a play in relation to a particular religious festival restricted to a limited number of days each year.

As can be seen then, the ancient and modern experience of theatre differed enormously. Some plays were written to reflect upon current events and when read as literary works it is important to always bear in mind how they were intended to be received by their original audiences, and in what context they were performed.

### Characteristics of the Greek theatre

The design of ancient Greek theatres is iconic and today modern cinemas and theatre halls still greatly resemble those initial theatres designed and built by the Ancient Greeks.

Theatres were constructed outdoors and to a similar design.

Several of these theatres still survive today, with the most famous being the theatre of Dionysius at Athens and the theatre at the sanctuary of Epidaurus, which now attract tens of thousands of tourists each year. These theatres are still in use and it is possible to see plays performed in them throughout the summer in Greece.

Theatre performances were probably restricted to a few special occasions a year. However smaller theatres at small towns such as Brauron in Attica were probably used by the local town councils for meetings also. Some theatres could accommodate a large number of people; the theatre of Dionysus in Athens for example can hold up to 14,000 people, as could the theatre at Epidaurus.

Theatre-going was not an activity limited to a particular social class. All ancient Greeks viewed theatre going as an activity available to them. However it is probable that women were excluded from some performances or from the seating provided and therefore had to content themselves with viewing the performances from a distance. If women could view the performances from a distance then it is also likely that slaves could do the same.

Greek tragedy conformed to certain genre expectations: it was staged on a vast scale, and took as its subject matter the ancient Greek myths as a starting point. The audience watching a tragedy were taking part in a communal experience, since the subject on stage was based on their shared cultural heritage.

Each play would also utilise props and scenic furniture as appropriate.

The design of a Greek theatre of an angled semi-circle was intentional. The acoustics of the design were so good, that if you dropped a coin in the orchestra, then the highest audience member sitting on the top tier might be able to hear it.

Today, many tourists create impromptu speeches at the theatre of Epidaurus which can be clearly heard by all present within the theatre. In modern film the emphasis is often on the visual impact of the film. In Ancient Greece it was most important that everybody could *hear* the play.

### The Theatre

The Greek theatre is easily identifiable as an outdoor structure of a semi-circular design. The audience sat on tiers in a semi-circle around a circular performance area, called an *orchestra*. There were two exits or entrances opposite the audience, leading to a building (*skéné*) which incorporated a stage platform and a roofed structure. This was the only roofed construction in the entire theatre: it served as a changing space for the cast of the play, but also where necessary could stand for a palace or house (as in the case of *Medea*) or even with decorative screens as a forest.

### The Theatre of Dionysius at Athens

The theatre at the base of the Acropolis in Athens is still in existence and is visited daily by tourists today. It could seat some 14,000 people; most would have been Athenian male citizens. However, there is evidence in the ancient sources that suggests that foreign visitors, women, children and slaves could watch the performances (Plato *Gorgias* 520d). Priests and city officials had reserved seats at the very front and in comic plays these dignitaries could be easily identified and targeted with a witty joke at the whim of the playwright.

**The theatre comprised the following;**

- Auditorium – seating area.
- Orchestra – dance floor where the chorus generally performed.
- Skene – originally a dressing room, but a building decorated with a façade with three doors. It was a two storey structure and often used as a prop in the play with actors using both floors and the doors to entry and exit as required.
- Raised platform – The stage were the actors performed. This was a wooden platform in front of the skene and including steps down to the orchestra.
- Parados – passageways between the skene and the auditorium used for entry and exit of the chorus.

**A vase painting depicting a *skéné***

### Stage Machinery and Props

The stage machinery used in the Ancient Greek theatre was fairly simplistic. Trapdoors were used for actors to access the stage from below. One of the main pieces of machinery was a large crane, called a *mechané*. The *mechané* was used to 'swing' actors and thus give the impression that they were flying. This was used especially when the play incorporated a god. If the god did not stand atop the *skéné* (stage building) or in the orchestra, then they could be moved around by the *mechané* to give the impression of flight.

This *mechané* may have been used by Medea in the Exodus of this play in order to transport her across the skies. It may be however that Medea remained in a model of her chariot atop the *skene*

Another important piece of equipment was the *ekkyklema*, a kind of wheeled, moveable platform that could be rolled on stage to display something; typically a 'dead' body.

Each play would also utilise various props and scenic furniture as appropriate. In *Medea*, important props would include the gown and crown sent to Glauce by Medea.

**Task: Understanding the Theatre**

*Make sure you understand the following definitions;*

- *orchestra*

- *skéné*

- *mechané*

- *ekkyklema*

### Athenian Dramatic Festivals

In common with the other kinds of theatrical genres of ancient Greece, Tragedy was performed as part of a religious festival or ceremony in honour of the god, Dionysus. In this, ancient and modern theatre are greatly at odds, the ancient theatre and religion were inexorably intertwined.

Tragedy, alongside the other genres, was performed only at two major festivals every year.

The first, in Athens, was the **City or Great Dionysia**, which took place over a few days in spring. The tragedies and the other types of theatre were performed as part of a mass competition in honour of the God Dionysus. This was a grand occasion; normal business was suspended and all citizens attended the festival for the purpose of watching the theatre on offer. Visitors from across the Greek world would also attend.

The second, the **Lenaia**, taking place probably earlier in the year, in January, was a less important festival. Although the festival was still to honour the god Dionysus, the plays performed tended towards comedy, rather than tragedy.

Both festivals were important religious events and the Athenian state took a great role and pride in preparing these enterprises. A senior official, called an *archon*, was put in charge of the *City Dionysia* and chose the three separate poets whose works would be entered for performance. He was also in charge of finding and allocating the actors.

### The Nature of competition at the *City(Great) Dionysia*

The three successful playwrights chosen by the *archon* in advance of the Great Dionysia were each allotted a *choregos*, or a rich citizen, whose role was to finance the production personally. The role of *choregos* was a voluntary form of civic duty undertaken by rich citizens as an alternative form of taxation; they could chose this role or that of equipping the Athenian navy as another way of performing the functions required of the city-state of Athens.

However, there were benefits for a *choregos* besides paying his taxes: spending money on a lavish and exciting new production would confer fame on him and hopefully would garner him popularity as well. For rich citizens with an eye on their political status on a public stage, this could be extremely useful. In other cities that did not have the resources of festivals of Athens, the rich would compete and demonstrate their wealth through the ownership of horses and chariot racing teams, as well as other spectacles, including provision of public buildings or dedications to the gods.

The Great Dionysia took place over five days. On three days of the festival, one playwright would present a trilogy of tragedies followed by a 'satyr' play, which was a kind of light-hearted farce, named after the mythological creature of the satyr. The three plays in the tragedy may have been linked by theme or not, but the only surviving complete trilogy we have is that of Aeschylus' *Oresteia*. This is composed of the plays *Agamemnon*, *Choephori* and *Eumenides*. A comedy would also be performed the same day.

### Task: Comparing and contrasting theatre plans

*Below are plans of two different theatres. One is a large theatre in Athens; the other was built to serve a much smaller community at Thorikos in Attica*

*Examine the plans and identify key differences and similarities between these plans*

*In what ways do they differ? In what ways are they the same?*

*Theatre of Dionysius at Athens*

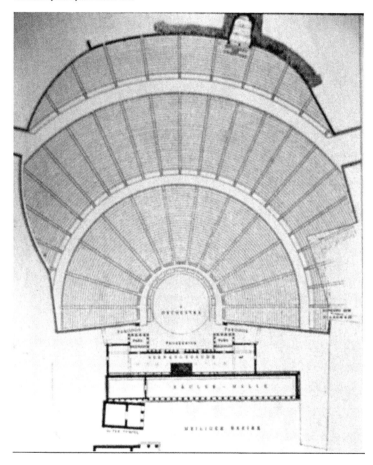

**Theatre at Thorikos Attica**

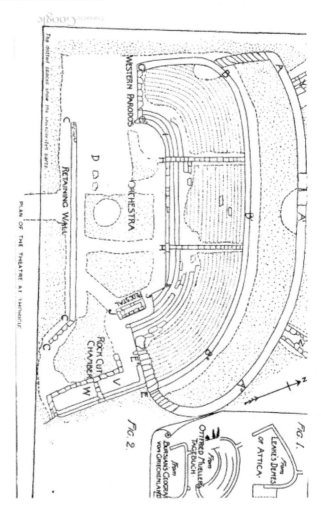

### The Structure of Greek Tragedy

Most tragic dramas open with a *Prologue* as monologue. In the case of Euripides' *Women of Troy* for example, it is the speech of Poseidon that begins the play. After the *Prologue*, usually the chorus enters and offers the *first* of the choral songs called the *Parados*. In the case of *Women of Troy*, Euripides inserts the first episode, consisting of the dialogue between Poseidon and Athena, between the *Prologue* and the *Parados*. The final scene is called the *Exodos*.

*Medea* follows a similar structure. The Prologue is a monologue from the Nurse; a peripheral character of the play who observes the impending tragedy. The Parados is innovative; consisting of the Chorus, the Nurse and interjections from Medea who is offstage.

The structure of Greek Tragedies often resembles the following;

*Prologue*

*Parados (Strophé / Antistrophé / Epodé)*

*First Episode*

*First Stasimon (Strophé / Antistrophé / Epodé)*

*Second Episode*

*Second Stasimon (Strophé / Antistrophé / Epodé)*

*Third Episode*

*Third Stasimon (Strophé / Antistrophé / Epodé)*

*Fourth Episode*

*Fourth Stasimon (Strophé / Antistrophé / Epodé)*

*Exodus*

---

## 1.2: The role and function of the Chorus and actors

This section will help you to;

- *Explain the use of actors and the Chorus in Greek tragedy.*

- *Explain ancient Greek dramatic terminology and conventions for both Chorus and actors.*

### The Use of the Chorus

The Chorus is a distinctive and perhaps the most important feature of the Greek Tragedy. The Chorus formed a centerpiece of the spectacle at the festival of Dionysius at Athens. Many plays, both comic and tragic, take their name from the chorus; for example *Women of Troy, Knights, Birds* and *Bacchae*.

To raise and train a Chorus was considered to be a great public duty and honour. As a result of the expense involved it was the wealthiest citizens who could afford to do this. The *chorégos* (Chorus leader) recruited, trained and costumed the chorus.

Despite the shift to an increased number of actors with speaking parts, the Chorus was an integral part of the drama and spectacle of a tragedy. The Chorus was made up of fifteen members, including a Chorus leader. Originally there were twelve members of a tragic chorus; later in the 5th century this was increased to fifteen. In contrast, comedies had a twenty four strong chorus and there were fifty in the chorus for a dithyramb.

The Chorus dance, sing and speak either in unison, in groups or individually through the Chorus leader, who might speak directly to the actors on stage. Besides these functions the Chorus served other important roles in the play. The dialogue spoken by the main actors (usually called 'episodes') was often punctuated by the choral songs or dances. This allowed the action to be slowed and indicate the passing of time, to act as 'scene changes' or to allow for a change of mood. The Chorus would also interject with lines in the dialogue of the main actors.

Furthermore, the choral songs allowed for some added variety to the format of the tragedy; the Chorus sang in a different type of verse to the spoken parts and so allowed the tragedian to demonstrate his skills of versification. These songs were often timed to the movement of the chorus about the performance area.

These lines, known as *strophé* and *antistrophé* ended with turns in direction made by the chorus as they sang and danced. These 'turns' and 'counterturns', combined with song, were an important in the context of performance; the tragedies were performed as part of a competition sacred to Dionysus and impressing the judges and audience was therefore paramount.

---

**The Use of Actors in Greek Tragedy**

The total number of actors with speaking parts started at one, and grew to two, finally stopping at three. A reason for limiting the number to three was probably practical. The audience may have been too distracted by too much occurring on stage at once and by several parts being played by the same actor who wore masks to identify these characters probably made additional speaking actors unnecessary.

Aristotle credited Aeschylus with adding the second actor and Sophocles with the third. This did not mean that tragedies had to be written with only three speaking parts; actors usually took more than one part. Besides the speaking parts, Greek tragedy also made use of walk-on, non-speaking parts, such as guards and slaves. In the *Antigone* for example a boy accompanies Tiresias on stage and is commented upon; yet has no lines.

The role of the speaking or non-speaking parts played by single actors grew in importance as the number of speaking-part actors was increased to three.

In Euripides' *Medea*, there are only ever two speaking actors onstage at any given time. There are a number of silent parts (the children, for example).

### Rhesis, Agon, Stichomythia, Kommos: Terminology relating to the Actors' Speech

As is expected in any play actors recite their lines. However, it is possible to identify particular styles of Actors' speech in Greek Tragedy. Below are the most common kinds of speech used in Greek tragedy;

- *Rhesis*
- *Stichomythia*
- *Agon*
- *Kommos*

### Rhesis

The *Rhesis* is the name given to a set speech by an actor which is characterised by logical argument or ordered reasoning, yet may also include emotional appeal. It could be a monologue, where a character reflects on his opinions, feelings and motivations, or it could be part of a dialogue or argument. It is a common feature of Greek Tragedy.

### Stichomythia

The *Stichomythia* is a particular kind of argument or dialogue, consisting of a rapid, single-line exchange between actors. It is not the only kind of dialogue in tragedy, but is of a highly distinctive kind. It serves to concentrate and heighten the emotion or argument, since the exchange frequently takes place between two characters of opposing view-points or of wildly different intentions.

### Agon

An *Agon* Identified as a set debate, another common feature. One character presents his or her case, in a formal manner, and another character refutes the points made. It has the feel of the 'law-court'. The aim is to capture the audience through reasoned argument, and since tragedies often represent the clash of two opposing ideologies, there is much food for thought to be found in the *Agon*

### Kommos

The *Kommos* is a lament. Often a *Kommos* is a lyrical exchange between the Chorus and a character, but can also be a monologue.

### Dramatic Conventions used in Greek Tragedy: The forms of Lyric poetry

### Iambic pentameter

The verse form of Greek Tragedy was a fundamental feature of the genre. The actors spoke in a type of verse called iambic pentameter, since this was considered to be the closest to normal speech. It has a rhythm of uniform metre that resembled *'te-tum, te-tum, te-tum'* in sound.

### Lyric poetry; *strophé, antistrophé* and *epode*

In origin lyric poetry and dance were an integral part of religious ceremony.

However, the choral songs were quite different, which again marked them off from the main spoken action. The type of poetry they sang in was called lyric poetry, and was of a far more complex kind than the verse of the actors with speaking parts. Choral songs were composed of three elements or 'stanzas'. These stanzas consisted of a number of turns and counterturns (*strophé* and *antistrophé*) as well as a different paced final stanza called the *'epode'*, which was of a different metrical pattern to the other two stanzas.

### Costume and Masks in Greek Tragedy

Besides the theatre building, scene machinery and Chorus, there were many other distinct features of Greek tragedy. All actors wore costumes and masks, although it is difficult to know exactly what design or type these took.

The masks were of rigid construction, with an aperture (opening) for the mouth. These masks were worn for a variety of reasons; firstly, the design of the theatre itself necessitated them. The aperture may have acted as a sound amplifier, helping the audience to hear the words he spoke or sang. The mask was also an exaggerated face and so would help the audience in the highest seats distinguish one part from another. The masks would also be in the form of stereotypes of stock characters, such as a King, an old man or a noble woman. This had the effect of clarifying from a distance which character was which.

*Red-figure Pelike by the Phiale Painter depicting tragic actors dressing*

**Task: Understanding tragedy**

*What can this vase painting tell us about Greek Theatre?*

*In the exam you will be required to explore images like the one above and scrutinise them for what they reveal about the Greek theatre.*

### Dramatic Conventions used in Greek Tragedy: The use of offstage action and the Messenger Speech

Greek tragedy also involved elements that were absent from the stage and performance area and yet were integral parts of the plot. In *Medea,* for example, the deaths of Glauce and Creon do not occur in view of the audience. Neither do the deaths of the children.

In modern day films, graphic killings and disturbing scenes are often used to shock and scare the audience. In the Ancient Greek theatre however graphic killings on stage were considered taboo at a religious festival. Nonetheless, they need to happen, and so Euripides uses other methods and techniques in order to inform the audience of these events.

### Off-stage Events

Examples of Tragic episodes and the demonstration of these events that occur 'off-stage' include;

- *Cries and distress*
- *Violence*
- *Description of events that have occurred or will occur*
- *Messenger Speeches*

### Cries and distress

In several plays; including Sophocles' *Ajax* and Euripides' *Medea* and *Electra,* a character may be heard crying or screaming off stage. This is used to increase tension.

### Violence

The portrayal of violence was taboo at a religious festival. Several Greek tragedies have violent episodes, including this one – but they are not portrayed onstage. When Clytemnestra and Aegisthus are murdered in *Electra*; it is done off stage and reported to the actors, chorus and audience by use of a Messenger. Likewise the deaths of Creon and Glauce are revealed through the use of a Messenger speech in *Medea.*

### Description of events that have occurred or will occur

Sometime news is delivered of important events that have occurred; such as the mysterious burial of the dead Polynieces in Sophocles' *Antigone*.

In this case the event is usually described by a Messenger, guard or other witness who comes on stage briefly to inform the actors and chorus of these distant events.

In *Medea*, the Tutor arrives onstage early in the play to announce that Medea is to be exiled. This reporting of events removes the element of surprise from the audience but does help the plot to advance at a rapid pace. Creon then can enter stage and immediately order Medea into exile.

### *The Messenger speech*

In contrast to the reasoned argument characteristic of the *Rhesis* or the *Agon*, the Messenger Speech makes full use of appeal to the audience's emotions.

These speeches are used as a reporting device of the tragedians, and allowed them to describe the violence vividly, a consequence of their characters' actions, without breaking the taboo of representing violence on-stage. The messenger speeches take the form of narrative; a messenger arrives to report on what he has seen take place out of sight of the audience.

---

*Task: Understanding tragedy: The Messenger Speech*

*The Messenger's Speech is often one of the most effective and moving events in a Greek Tragedy.*

Why do you think that this might be the case?

---

## 1.3: Aristotle and Tragedy

This section will help you to;

- *Understand key concepts of Greek Tragedy as defined by Aristotle.*

- *Explain the use of actors and the Chorus in Greek theatre.*

- *Explain ancient Greek dramatic terminology and conventions for both Chorus and actors.*

### Who was Aristotle?

Aristotle was a Greek philosopher born at Stagira, in Northern Greece, in 384BC. As a young man, Aristotle journeyed to Athens and studied under the philosopher Plato before moving to Macedonia in order to become the tutor of Alexander the Great in 343BC. Aristotle wrote many works, including studies of science, philosophy and politics, some of these works survive to this day. One of his most famous pieces of writings was the *Poetics*, in which Aristotle defines and explains Greek literature, including Greek tragedy. Unfortunately, Aristotle's work on comedy has not survived.

### Key concepts of Greek tragedy as defined by Aristotle

These terms, used by Aristotle in his work on the nature of Greek tragedy, called the *Poetics,* are very useful to our understanding of tragedy.

Aristotle himself states the following about Greek tragedy;

*VI.2 A tragedy...is the imitation of an action that is serious...in a dramatic, not in a narrative form; with incidents arousing pity and fear, with which to accomplish its catharsis of such emotions...*

*IX.11-12 Tragedy is an imitation ...of incidents arousing pity and fear. Such incidents have the very greatest effect on the mind when they occur unexpectedly and at the same time in consequence of one another; they arouse more awe than if they happened accidentally and by chance...*

Our own understanding and reasons for enjoying films today is somewhat different from what an Ancient Greek would think about a Greek theatrical performance. Modern audiences often go to see films because they admire a particular actor or a particular genre, such as horror or romance. Neither may have excited an Ancient Athenian. Actors wore masks and were generally of low or even, by Roman times, disreputable status. Athenians also only had a few broad genres – tragedy, comedy and satyr plays for example.

There are similarities, however. Often we enjoy a film because it stirs our emotions – it scares or excites us. We might find a film funny or we might admire the script and scene.

## Criteria for a Tragedy from Aristotle's *Poetics*

According to Aristotle elsewhere in his writings, a Greek Tragedy must contain the following;

- Imitation of reality (*mimesis*)
- A plot with serious implications
- Be complete and coherent and possesses magnitude
- Utilise sophisticated language and enactment
- Purification (*catharsis*)

## Imitation of reality (*mimesis*)

Aristotle argues that the artist does not just copy the shifting appearances of the world, but rather imitates or represents reality itself, and gives form and meaning to that reality. In so doing, the artist gives shape to the universal, not the accidental.

## A plot with serious implications

The plot must be serious in the sense that it best raises and purifies pity and fear, as well as serious in a moral, psychological, and social sense.

## Be complete and coherent and possesses magnitude

A tragedy must be complete and coherent, just a series of episodes, but also contain a beginning, a middle, and an end. The idea of imitation is important here; the artist does not just slavishly copy everything related to an action, but selects (represents) only those aspects which give form to universal truths.

### Utilise sophisticated language and enactment

Language must be appropriate for each part of the play: choruses are in a different meter and rhythm and more melodious than spoken parts. Tragedy also relies on an enactment (dramatic performance), not on "narrative" (the author telling a story).

### Purification (*catharsis*)

A Greek tragedy must first raise the emotions of pity and fear, and then purify or purge them.

> ### Task: Aristotle's criteria of Tragedy
>
> *Which of these do you think is the most important criteria?*
> *Write a few paragraphs explaining why you think that one*
> *or more criteria are more important than another.*

**Key concepts of Greek tragedy as defined by Aristotle:**

*Hamartia, Catharsis and Peripeteia*

These three terms, used by Aristotle in his work on the nature of Greek tragedy, called the *Poetics,* are very useful to our understanding of tragedy. These are;

- *Hamartia*
- *Peripeteia*
- *Katharsis*

*Hamartia*

*Hamartia* derives from a Greek root word meaning 'to miss the mark' or 'to fall short'. In the context of Greek tragedy, *hamartia* refers to a failing of the central character which brings about the catastrophe. It has sometimes been translated as a 'character flaw'; but this is to fall short of the true meaning of the word.

In fact, it is not so much an in-grained character fault as more an opportunity missed, or bad decision made which sets up the inescapability and inevitability of the tragic events which follow. Each tragedy possesses this 'falling short' or *Hamartia,* of a central character, and will be considered in our close reading of the text.

An example of *Hamartia* in *Medea* is the failure of Creon to exile Medea immediately. He comes across as arrogant and bullying and yet becomes at the end of the first episode indecisive; Medea succeeds in manipulating Creon into allowing her to delay her exile for one day; enough time for the events of the tragedy to unfold and for Medea to enact her revenge.

*Peripeteia*

*Peripeteia* refers to a (usually sudden) reversal or change of fortune of the central character. Again, like *hamartia* this is a typical feature of a Greek tragedy. The reversal can be from good to bad or vice versa. Aristotle considered the first, the change from happiness to misery, the more significant for tragedy.

Jason rapidly undertakes a reversal of fortunes in *Medea*. He arrives on stage a man making his way upwards in Corinthian Society; he ends the play a broken man with no family and no home.

### *Katharsis*

*Katharsis* gives us our word 'cathartic' which we use to refer to something with a great cleansing or purging power. The word in the context of Greek tragedy refers to the effect a 'good' tragedy should have on the audience. It should purge the audience of its emotions, by inducing feelings such as pity, anger or fear and allowing the audience a safe place for the expression of them.

A cathartic event in the Euripides' *Electra* is the appearance of the Dioscoûri at the end of the play. Both Orestes and Electra are contaminated by their actions. They need to be cleansed and the gods explain how this can be achieved. In *Medea* however, Euripides denies his audience this sense of *Katharsis*.

---

**Aristotle on Peripeteia**

*X.1-3 Plots are either simple or complex, since the actions they represent naturally are characterized by a similar difference. The action, proceeding in the way defined, as one continuous whole, I call simple, when the change in the hero's fortune takes place without peripeteia ('reversal of fortune') or discovery; and complex, when it involves one or the other, or both. These should each of them arise out of the structure of the plot itself, so as to be the consequence, necessary or probable, of the preceding action. It makes a great difference whether what happens is caused by the preceding action of just follows it.*

*XI.1-5 A peripeteia is the change of the kind described from one state of things within the plot to its opposite, and that too in the way we are saying, in accordance with probability or necessity; as it is for instance in Oedipus; here the opposite state of things is produced by the Messenger, who, coming to gladden Oedipus and to remove his fears as to his mother, reveals the secret of his birth...A discovery is, as the very word implies, a change from ignorance to knowledge, and thus to either love or hate, in the personages marked for good or evil fortune. The finest form of discovery is one attended by peripeteia, like that which goes with the discovery in Oedipus. There are no doubt other forms of it; what we have said may happen in a way in reference to discover whether someone has done or not done something. But the form most directly connected with the plot and the action is the first mentioned. This, with a peripeteia, will arouse either pity or fear-- actions of that nature being what Tragedy is assumed to represent; and it will also serve to bring about the happy or unhappy ending. The discovery, then, being of persons, it may happen that one person only is recognized by the other, the latter being already known, or it may be necessary that the recognition take place on both sides...*

---

> **Task: Aristotle**
>
> *Write yourself an explanation of tragedy and the importance of peripeteia as described by Aristotle.*

### Hamartia and the tragic hero

In addition to these criteria, Aristotle also states that a Greek Tragedy must have another essential feature: The Tragic Hero.

The Tragic Hero is according to Aristotle; *"a great man who is neither a paragon of virtue and justice nor undergoes the change to misfortune through any real badness or wickedness but because of some mistake (Hamartia)"*

*Hamartia: This Greek word has been translated as "flaw" or as "error."*

The great man falls through--though not entirely because of--some weakness of character, some moral blindness, or error. We should note that the gods also are in some sense responsible for the hero's fall.

Finally, according to Aristotle, a Greek Tragedy must encompass the following plot devices;

For Aristotle the plot is the most important characteristic of a tragedy. For Aristotle, the best tragic plots contain the following key features;

- *Peripeteia*
- *Anagnorisis*
- *Pathos*

**Reversal (*peripeteia*):**

> Occurs when a situation seems to developing in one direction, and then suddenly "reverses" to another.

**Recognition (*anagnorisis*):**

> A change from ignorance to awareness of a bond of love or hate. For example, Oedipus kills his father in ignorance and then learns of his true relationship to the King of Thebes. Recognition scenes in tragedy are of some horrible event or secret, while those in comedy usually reunite long-lost relatives or friends. A plot with tragic reversals and recognitions best arouses pity and fear.

**Evokes sympathy or pity (*pathos*):**

> Represents an appeal to the emotions of the audience, and elicits feelings that already reside in them. This third element of plot is a destructive or painful act that evokes pity.

---

*Task: Understanding tragic definitions.*

*Ensure that you understand the following tragic definitions;*

- *Anagnorisis*
- *Catharsis*
- *Hamartia*
- *Mimesis*
- *Pathos*
- *Peripeteia*

---

## PART TWO: Euripides' *Medea*

## 2.1 Introduction

This section will help you to;

- *Understand the structure Euripides' Medea.*

- *Explore the character and myth of Medea.*

- *Begin to explore the other characters in the play.*

**Structural overview of Euripides' *Medea***

Below is an outline of the plot and structure of *Medea*.

- **The *Prologue***
  (Lines 1-130): The Nurse and the Tutor with Medea offstage
- **The *Parados* of the Chorus**
  (Lines 131-213) Chorus with interjections from the Nurse and Medea offstage
- **1st Episode: Medea and Creon**
  (Lines 214-414)
- **1st Choral Ode**
  (Lines 415-446)
- **2nd Episode: Medea and Jason**
  (Lines 447-629)
- **2nd Choral Ode**
  (Lines 630-660)
- **3rd Episode: Medea and Aegeus**
  (Lines 661-839)
- **3rd Choral Ode**
  (Lines 840-867)
- **4th Episode: Medea and Jason**
  (Lines 868-976)
- **4th Choral Ode**
  (Lines 977-1001)
- **5th Episode: Medea and Tutor (Medea's *kommos*)**
  (Lines 1002-1081)
- **5th Choral Ode**
  (Lines 1082-1117)
- **6th Episode: Medea and the Messenger's Speech**
  (Lines 1118-1251)
- **6th Choral Ode**
  (Lines 1252-1323)
- **Exodus : Medea and Jason**
  (Lines 1324-1419)

At a glance there are several things that are apparent.

First of all, Medea is present in every episode of the play. Once Medea comes on stage at the beginning of the first episode she remains on stage throughout. However Medea is also a feature of both the *Prologue* and the *Parados*; she is not on stage, but nonetheless she is present as both the focus of the discussion of the Nurse, Tutor and the Chorus, but she also makes frequent interjections from offstage. The result then is that there is no part of Euripides' play that is free of Medea.

Secondly, each episode is a series of confrontations between Medea and male counterparts, and in each of these encounters, it is Medea that dominates proceedings and obtains the upper hand.

Thirdly, the Choral Odes in Medea are almost all short, consisting of around 30 lines on each occasion. The only exception to this is the 6th Choral Ode which is a little longer, but still brief in comparison to many other Greek Tragedies.

As we progress with our exploration of *Medea*, we will go into greater detail on each of these episodes and the role of the chorus throughout.

### *Dramatis Personae* in *Medea*

Nurse – a household slave of Medea and Jason
Tutor – a household slave of Medea and Jason
The Children – the two male children of Medea and Jason
Medea – a foreign woman with divine origins
Creon – The King of Corinth
Jason – A Hero
Aegeus – The King of Athens
Messenger – delivering news
The Chorus – Corinthian Women

### Medea – the Mythical traditions of Medea

Medea was the daughter of Aeétés, the King of Colchis. Colchis was a kingdom thought to be on the coast of the Black Sea (probably somewhere near modern day Georgia) and therefore a land far distant from mainland Greece and known mostly through myth only. However, by the mid-5th century, the Athenians had expanded their trading base into the Black Sea and relied on the Black Sea trade to help feed the population of the city. However, the Black Sea was home to several 'barbaric' realms and peoples.

Colchis then was considered by the Greeks to be a barbarian kingdom and as it was located in Asia, was somewhat equated with the Persian Empire.

Medea was a barbarian princess, but she was more than that. Her grandfather was Helios, the Sun God and her aunt was Circe, a Goddess whom Odysseus encountered during the *Odyssey*. Medea was in myth a demi-Goddess; a granddaughter of the Sun; one of the most powerful of all Gods, and like her aunt Circe, Medea was a sorceress knowledgeable in drugs, poisons and enchantments.

In Hesiod, Medea is depicted as an immortal and according to another myth, when she died she married Achilles and lived with him in Elysium.

Medea is most famous however for her association with Jason and the Argonaut Quest. When Jason and the Argonauts reach Colchis Medea provides invaluable help to Jason. She helps him kill the Serpent that guarded the Golden Fleece and helped Jason to escape the pursuit of the Colchians by murdering her own brother Apsyrtus (who was either a baby or a young man). Seeing her kill her brother, Aeétés halted the pursuit in order to collect his remains.

On arrival in Jason's homeland of Iolcus, Medea and Jason married and had children. Medea is credited with rejuvenating the aged father of Jason and then fooling Pelias' daughters into murdering him, in order to make Pelias young again.

After the death of Pelias, Medea and Jason fled Iolcus to the city of Corinth (where Euripides' takes up the story of Medea and Jason). Jason then left Medea in order to marry Glauce, the princess of Corinth.

In some myths Medea then took revenge, murdering Glauce and Creon and either the Corinthians murdered her children in retaliation, or else Medea killed the children in a failed attempt to make them immortal. Euripides' tale, however, takes a twist on this story; rather than the Corinthians killing the children of Medea and Jason, Medea kills the boys herself. Medea's children were certainly an object of religious cult in Corinth and worshipped on the Acrocorinth (the mountain/acropolis above the city itself).

Medea then fled to Athens and married the Athenian king Aegeus, but was exiled again after she tried to poison Theseus.

**Medea and the Serpent that guards the Golden Fleece**

## 2.2: The *Prologue*

This section will help you to;

- *Understand the first part of Euripides' Medea.*

- *Explore the character of the Nurse.*

- *Begin to explore the character of the Tutor.*

- *Introduce some of the themes explored in this play.*

- *Consider the role of slaves in Greek society as seen through Tragedy.*

- *Begin to explore language techniques employed by Euripides.*

- *Begin to explore some Greek terminology relevant to Tragedy.*

---

### The Prologue

Many of Euripides' dramas open with a *Prologue,* which takes the form as a monologue, and *Medea* follows this basic structure with a few elaborations.

The Prologue consists mainly of a monologue from the Nurse, a peripheral character of the play who observes the impending tragedy. However, the Nurse is also joined on stage by another peripheral character, the Tutor, and from offstage Medea can be heard crying out in fury and distress at her situation.

> **Task: Plotting the course of the play**
>
> To what extent is the plot of Euripides' Medea mapped out in the prologue?
>
> Consider what events are alluded to in the prologue and what events are not revealed in this part of the play.

### The Nurse (lines 1-48)

**Key term - Metaphor**

*A metaphor is a figure of speech that compares a subject to another which is otherwise unrelated. Comparing your life to a journey is a metaphor, or like Shakespeare in his play 'As you like it';*

*"All the world is a stage,*

*And all the men and women merely players;*

*They have their exits and their entrances"*

The first lines of Euripides' *Medea* are spoken by the Nurse. The Nurse is a minor character but has the important duty of explaining the immediate context of the play and also of explaining the predicament that Medea is in at the beginning of the play.

The Nurse's opening lines are ones of sorrow and regret; *"If only they had never gone!..."* and it is in these themes that the Nurse explains the immediate context.

If the Argonauts had never set sail, had the *Argo* never even been built, then Pelias would not have sent Jason and the Argonauts to Colchis to obtain the Golden Fleece. If this had never happened then Jason would not have fallen in love with Medea and returned with her to Greece. Pelias would not have been killed by Medea's trickery and Jason, Medea and their children would never have come to live in Corinth.

Nurse then goes onto to explain the more immediate situation to the audience. Jason has abandoned Medea and their two sons in order to marry the Princess Glauce, daughter of Creon, king of Corinth. Medea is both enraged and in despair and is so distraught by Jason's actions that she refuses to eat or to listen to the reason of her friends.

Euripides has the Nurse employ a metaphor in lines 27-28 to help explain Medea's stubbornness;

*"she might be a rock or wave of the sea for all she hears"*

**Task: Comprehending the Nurse's speech**

*What is the Nurse's attitude towards Medea, her situation and her attitude towards Jason in lines 1-48?*

The Nurse's speech in lines 1-48 introduces three major themes that are explored in greater detail throughout the play;

- The theme of Women and their place in Ancient Greek society
- The theme of Foreigners and their place in Ancient Greek society
- The theme of Medea's violent and dangerous nature

We will explore each of these themes in greater detail later on.

### Nurse and the Tutor (lines 49-87)

**Key term – Simile**

A *simile* is a common literary technique that is a comparison of one item with another with which it intentionally similar. Generally speaking if something is like something else then this is a simile. So for example in Euripides' *Medea* the Nurse likens Medea to a lion or a wild bull.

With the Nurse ending her speech with the warning that Medea is a dangerous woman who will not easily be defeated by anyone who makes an enemy of her, the Nurse is now joined on stage by three character, the Tutor and two children (who do not speak ever on stage).

The Tutor arrives and asks the Nurse what she is doing and why she is not in attendance on Medea.

Medea's grief is explored briefly in the exchange that follows, but the main reason for the arrival of the Tutor on stage is twofold;

- To bring news of more calamity for Medea
- To present to the audience the children of Jason and Medea

The Tutor is bringing news and this news is bad. Medea has not only been abandoned by Jason, but worse still, Medea and her children are to be exiled this very day by Creon, king of Corinth.

The Nurse briefly hopes that Jason will intervene and prevent his own children from being exiled.

This hope is soon quashed by the Tutor who states that;

> *"Jason is no friend to this house (oikos)"*

Nurse and Tutor decide not to tell Medea.

The Nurse then takes over the bulk of the lines. The Nurse is wary of Medea's attitude towards her children. She fears that Medea will cause them harm. Euripides employs a simile here in line 91;

> *"I've seen her watching them, her eye like a wild bull's"*

The employment of this simile is to illustrate that Medea is not to be trusted; that she is dangerous and that caution is needed around her – just like you would when confronted by a wild bull.

The Nurse's final line (line 94) before Medea's first offstage interjection is a prayer;

> *"God grant she strike her enemies and not her friends"*

The presence of the children on stage at this point is crucial as it underpins future events of the play and highlights the dangerous nature of Medea. The audience are forewarned by Euripides that the children are in danger from their mother.

The Tutor and the children exit the stage and the Nurse raises again her concerns for the children. Why should the children suffer for the wicked actions of their father?

### Slavery in the Ancient World

Both the Tutor and the Nurse are slaves.

Slavery was an integral part of Ancient Greek society and to be a slave was both commonplace and a potential fate to any citizen of a Greek city (*polis*).

*Key terms: Oikos and Oiketai*

*Oikos – the Ancient Greek house and social building block upon which Ancient Greek society was built.*

*Oiketai – Household slaves*

Whilst it is impossible to be accurate, it has been plausibly estimated that perhaps 25-50% of the total population of Athens in the mid-5th century was slaves. This meant that out of a total population of some around 250,000 individuals – some 80-125,000 were slaves in 431BC.

There were many different kinds of slaves in Athenian society. Some were owned by the state, some were owned by individuals. Some were employed as private servants, others treated like animals in the mines, whilst still others had positions of great responsibility in Athens.

The most important slaves were the state owned slaves that possessed skills required for specialized professions. These included official coin testers and court clerks. Also of note were the Scythian archers – a body of slaves that served as a kind of police force.

Privately owned slaves could live in their own homes and ran their own businesses – such as metal workers. Some of these slaves were expensive to own. The Athenian politician and general Nicias purchased a slave to oversee and run a sliver mine for the huge price of 1000 talents.

At the bottom end of slave hierarchy were the slaves employed as agricultural workers, or worse still, as slaves in the silver mines of Attica. Their lives could be brutal and short.

Somewhere in between were the *'oiketai'*, the household slaves, and it is in this class of slaves that the Nurse and the Tutor fall. These slaves were an integral part of the Greek household (*oikos*) and were companions and assistants for the husband and wife, but also played an important role in raising the children.

### The common sense attitudes of slaves

In Greek Theatre (both in Tragedy and Comedy), some of the most intelligent and sensible characters are slaves. Nurse and to a lesser extent Tutor, are no exception to this trend. Nurse's final lines in the Prologue (lines 122-129) to the entry of the Chorus are a warning to the audience to live a simple life of neither austerity nor excess. This is the way to avoid the anger of the Gods.

The Ancient Greeks used the word *'sophrosyne'* which means self-control or temperance and it is *sophrosyne* that the Nurse urges the audience to pursue.

When sophrosyne was not obtained, the Ancient Greeks would use another word; *'akolasia'* which means 'uncorrected excess'. *Akolasia* would occur when moralistic excess (particularly desire) was not corrected by the application of reason.

---

*Key term: Akolasia*

*Akolasia is a Greek term for 'Uncorrected'. It is commonly defined as a moralistic term which occurs when desires are not corrected by the application of reason.*

*The failure to correct Medea's anger through reason leads to disaster in this play.*

---

*Key term: Sophrosyne*

*Sophrosyne is a Greek term for 'Self-Control' or Temperance. It is commonly defined as a harmonious state of rational control of desires. Sophrosyne was considered to be a cardinal virtue of the Ancient Greeks and the absence of Sophrosyne in Greek Tragedies usually leads to disaster for those concerned.*

---

*Task: Contrasting views of the prologue*

*Write a brief defence, consisting of two to three paragraphs, for each of the following statements;*

a) *Euripides' Medea is spoiled by the prologue because it provides the audience with too much information.*

b) *Euripides' Medea is enhanced by the wealth of themes introduced in the prologue.*

---

## 2.3: The *Parados*

This section will help you to;

• *Understand the entry of the Chorus into the play.*

• *Begin to understand the role and function of the Chorus in Euripides' Medea.*

• *Begin to explore the themes of Sophrosyne (Self Control) and Synome (Forgiveness) in Euripides' Medea.*

• *Begin to consider the importance of the oikos in Greek Society.*

• *Explore the unusual structure of the Parados in Euripides' Medea.*

### The *Parados*

Many of Euripides' Tragedies are structured somewhat differently from those of Sophocles and Aeschylus and in the *parados* of Medea we can see some of this innovation.

The *parados* traditionally was a Choral song; typically a highlight of the performance of the Tragedy. Here the audience would witness the arrival onstage of the Chorus and hear their opening song and witness their dance and costume.

However, in *Medea*, the Chorus entry is more dialogue than song that is interrupted by both the only actor currently on stage; Nurse, and also by the cries and lamentations of Medea off-stage. It is during the *parados* that the Nurse exits the stage and is replaced shortly after by Medea herself.

### Analysis of the *parados*

The Chorus in Medea consists of Corinthian Women and as local women, the Chorus sings of the grief of Medea and how this grief is turning to anger and also details her threats of violence against Jason and Glauce, his bride to be.

In the first verse the Chorus makes a request of the Nurse; they ask her to tell them about Medea's grief and the household *(oikos)* of Jason.

Nurse responds to the last request first (a stylistic technique commonly adopted in Homer in the *Odyssey* and the *Iliad*) and claims that Jason's *oikos* is no longer in existence - a brief foreshadowing of what course the play will take- and then responds briefly to the first question. Medea is inconsolable.

Medea then cries from off-stage. She is in despair and prays for death.

The Chorus then responds directly to Medea, even though she is offstage. Medea prays for death, the Chorus prays that she does not crave for madness and death.

Medea replies - still from off-stage. She invokes the Goddesses Themis and Artemis to help her seek revenge on Jason and his new bride. She has abandoned her own traditional *oikos* – she is far away from Colchis, having left her father and committed the crime of murdering her brother, all in the name of her love for Jason, who has now abandoned her in turn.

The Nurse then responds – there is no easy cure for Medea's rage and distress. The Chorus then responds to the Nurse. Perhaps Medea might listen to them, if only she will come forth. Perhaps they can reason with her.

The Nurse states that she will try to reason with Medea, though she fears it a fruitless task. The Nurse likens Medea to a wild bull, '*or a lioness guarding her cubs*'. As will soon be seen, this last simile is particularly ironic. As Medea is prepared to see her own children dead in order to achieve her revenge, she cannot be seen as particularly protective.

The Nurse's final lines are of songs. She questions why songs are not used to help sooth people's grief and anger. These final lines of Nurse before she leaves the stage help us to understand the Nurses' view of *sophrosyne* (self-control or temperance).

The *parados* ends with a few more lines from the Chorus. They return to the grief of Medea, how she has been wronged by Jason and how Medea prays to Themis, the hearer of prayers for assistance.

### The structure of the *parados*

The *parados* takes the following structure;

- Chorus (1st verse)
- Nurse
- Medea (offstage)
- Chorus (2nd verse)
- Medea (offstage)
- Nurse
- Chorus (3rd verse)
- Nurse (exits stage at the end of this verse)
- Chorus (final verse with Medea entering the stage)

The structure of this *parados* is unusual for a Greek Tragedy, but Euripides is known for playing with the structure of his *parados*. For example;

In Euripides' *Hecabe* the Chorus is much more traditional and consists of 50 lines of uninterrupted Choral Ode (lines 100-153). On the other hand, Euripides' *Electra* (lines 168-216) consists of the Chorus and Electra singing alternate verses (Chorus/ Electra/Chorus/Electra/Chorus).

*Task: Analyzing the parados*

*Explore the following questions:*

a) *To what extent might an Ancient Athenian audience find the parados of Medea a challenge to their expectations?*

b) *In what ways could we argue that the parados of Medea is both exciting and innovative?*

## 2.4: Exploring the First *Rhesis* of Medea

This section will help you to;

- *Begin to explore the character of Medea.*

- *Explore the character of Creon in this play.*

- *Begin to consider the role and function of women and marriage in Greek Society.*

- *Explore the nature of being a foreigner in a Greek polis.*

- *Consider the context in which Medea was first performed.*

### Medea's entry and First *Rhesis*

Medea enters the stage at the end of the *parados* and begins to speak on line 214. Medea has already undergone something of a transformation. So far she has been distraught and angered. But now she presents herself on stage, she is calm and rational.

Medea's first speech (*Rhesis*) is fairly extensive and includes discussion of several notable themes.

The discussion is of;

- Marriage, divorce and adultery
- The positions of men and women in Society
- The position of foreigners

Medea also announces that it is her intent to take revenge upon Jason and asks the Chorus not to tell anyone of what she intends. At the moment Euripides provides his audience with no information on the manner of this revenge – jut that it is Medea's desire to have it.

The First *Rhesis* of Medea is one of huge importance to understanding the context of the play as it was first performed in Athens in 431BC.

---

*Task: Analysing Medea's First Rhesis*

*Read Medea lines 214-268*

*What does this speech tell us about;*

- *Medea's character and personality*
- *Her views on women, marriage and being a foreigner?*

---

**The role of Women in Athens**

Pericles, in his funeral speech says that *'the greatest glory of a woman is to be least talked about by men'* (Thucydides, *History of the Peloponnesian War* 2.46).

Women were otherwise excluded from most public and political rights, as this quote indicates. The proper sphere for women, according to male Athenian general opinion, was inside the house where they should not live in a way that would attract gossip or malicious rumour to themselves.

The primary way in which women played a part in Athenian democracy was in their role as caregivers and mothers, the producers of the next generation of Athenian citizens.

Although this narrowed the role of women to a strictly biological one, intimately connected to their fertility and ability to procreate successfully, there is no doubt that women who produced a large and healthy family, including many sons, could gain prestige and honour in their social circle because of the importance of motherhood.

### Marriage

Marriage was primarily a contract, a process in which a man could beget children and descendants for his *oikos*. Marriages were not established for emotional reasons such as love, although feelings of affection and love no doubt were key factors in many, if not the majority, of Ancient Greek marriages.

Marriage could indeed be thought of as more of a transfer of ownership of a woman from one *oikos* (the father's) to that of another (the husband). The main aim was procreation and the husband was now granted control of the woman. The act of marriage also included the granting of gifts – money, property and livestock in the form of a dowry.

As stated above, the main purpose of marriage was to have children. If a woman failed to produce children (whether it was her fault or not) she was in danger of being divorced and replaced. Childbirth however was fraught with danger and was all too often fatal for both mother and child. It is probable that more women died in childbirth in Athens each year than did men in battle - hence Medea's lines 248-249;

*"Live free from danger, they go out to battle: fools!*

*I'd rather stand three times in the front line than bear one child"*

### Divorce

A marriage, like most other contracts, could be terminated. However, whereas today a woman is able to divorce a man, In Athens in the 5th Century only a man could decide if a divorce was to occur. The wife concerned had no say in the matter.

All the husband needed to do if he desired a divorce was to return the wife (and her dowry) to her original household.

### Adultery

In 5th Century Athens a man who was caught in the act of having sex with another man's wife, sister, daughter or mother could be killed legally under the law on the grounds of justifiable homicide. Alternatively the man so caught in the act could be held for ransom and released only on payment of an agreed sum of money or goods.

In practice this second option was probably more common since no-one would want the reputation of being a man whose own *oikos* had been violated.

Adulterous wives, on the other hand, had to be divorced immediately on legal grounds and were barred from participation in public sacrifices.

Unlike women, men had options if they desired extra-marital unions. They could visit a prostitute *('Hetairai')* legally and without stigma. They could also keep and maintain a concubine if they had the wealth and means.

### Aspasia- A dangerous foreign woman?

*One of the most famous concubines in Athens was a woman from the city of Megara called Aspasia. She had been living in Athens at least from the early 440s BC and was the concubine of Pericles, the foremost politician and statesman in Athens in the years 460-429BC.*

*Pericles had divorced his wife in the 440sBC and taken up living with Aspasia. Together they had at least one child, a son also named as Pericles – who was granted special dispensation to be recognized as a full Athenian citizen.*

*In the late 430s however Aspasia was legally prosecuted by opponents of Pericles because it was thought she had far too much influence over Pericles. When Athens went to war against the Peloponnesians in 431BC, the comic poet Aristophanes blamed this war in part on the intrigues of Aspasia.*

*Perhaps Euripides' wrote the Medea in part to warn the Athenians of the dangers of foreign women with excessive influence – like Aspasia.*

### Metics: Resident foreigners

*Metics* were resident foreigners. They take their name from the Greek word *'metoikos'* which means *'home changers'*.

The Athenians did not at all have a concept of universal human rights, as we would understand it in modern political theory; rather, their concept of rights was very much focussed on the *polis*. Since slaves were not free men of the *polis*, they had no rights (rather they were commodities to be traded); since women were not full citizens of the *polis* they were denied full rights and since *Metics*, though resident, were not native to the *polis*, they also were denied voting rights.

The exclusion of these large social groups was due to the Athenian concept of democratic rights as a privilege of free-born Athenian men only. In Athens in 451BC it became law that in order to qualify as a citizen of Athens; both parents had to be from Athenian *oikoi*. In practice this meant that marriage between an Athenian and a foreigner was prohibited.

However despite being denied the political rights of a citizen, these excluded groups still had some protections under law and served other important functions within Athenian public and political life. For example, *Metics* still had obligations to the city (since they lived in it), despite being non-Athenians. They were taxed (they had a particular kind of tax, called a *'Metic tax'*) and they had to take military service where necessary. In return, *Metics* were permitted to reside in Athens as their permanent home, and were given some legal rights, though they were required to have an Athenian citizen whom they nominated as their protector.

## 2.5: The First Episode: Medea and Creon

This section will help you to;

- *Begin to explore the character of Medea.*

- *Understand the character of Creon in this play.*

- *Understand Creon's Hamartia.*

- *Explore the first Agon in Medea.*

- *Continue to explore the mythical background of Medea.*

- *Continue to explore the contextual background of the year 431BC.*

### Creon

Creon, the King of Corinth, enters the stage and immediately orders Medea to leave Corinth. He states that he will not leave her presence until Medea and her sons have left Corinth. But as is clear; Creon fails in this.

Creon is responsible not only for the safety and wellbeing of his own *oikos*, but also for the safety and prosperity of Corinth as a whole. Creon then needs to be strong willed, decisive and have in the forefront of his mind the safety of his family and his city.

**Key term: Creon**

*We think of Creon as the name of the King of Corinth. There is another Creon in Thebes identified in legend through Sophocles' Antigone and Oedipus the King*

*In fact 'Creon' was a generic title that indicated 'lord' or 'ruler'.*

.

**Key term: Hamartia**

*Hamartia derives from a Greek root word meaning 'to miss the mark' or 'to fall short'. In the context of Greek tragedy, hamartia refers to a failing of the central character which brings about the catastrophe. It has sometimes been translated as a 'character flaw'; but this is to fall short of the true meaning of the word.*

### Creon and Medea

Medea asks why she is to be banished – what crime has she committed? Creon replies that Medea has committed no crime, but he is exiling her because he fears her (*Phobos*).

As events unfold during the play this fear is more than justified.

Creon states that Medea must be exiled because;

- He is afraid for the safety of Glauce
- Medea is intelligent
- Medea is angry and vengeful
- Medea has uttered threats against Jason, Glauce and Creon.

Creon's *Hamartia* is that he fails to carry out his intent to exile Medea. If he had succeeded in his stated aim then Medea would not be able to carry out her terrible acts.

> *Task: Medea and Creon*
>
> *Write responses to the following questions;*
>
> *What does this episode tell us about Medea's character?*
>
> *What does this episode tell us about Creon's character?*

### The importance of Fear in 431BC in Athens and in *Medea*

**Key term: Phobos**

*Fear*

Interestingly, these fears of Creon are similar to those stated by the Athenian Historian Thucydides as the real reason why the Peloponnesian War of 431-404BC started; through the Peloponnesians and Spartans fear of the strength of Athens and the Athenian Empire.

Shortly after *Medea* was performed, the Athenians and the Spartans and their allies declared war upon each other, and one of the primary allies of Sparta was the city of Corinth – who had been fighting a proxy war with Athens since 433BC.

Creon then exemplifies fear – he is knowledgeable of the threat faced, but he nonetheless underestimates the threat of Medea and in failing to respond as he should to this threat – Creon seals his own fate and that of his beloved daughter.

### The *Agon* of Creon and Medea

*Key term: Agon*

*An Agon identified as a set debate, another common feature. One character presents his or her case, in a formal manner, and another character refutes the points made. It has the feel of the 'law-court' about them*

Medea and Creon embark on an *Agon* – a set debate, with Medea acting as the defense and Creon the prosecution. Medea's first speech in this *Agon* is two part. The first part of this *Rhesis* (lines 291-315) is a defense of her own on intelligence and reputation. Her intelligence she argues is a curse – it makes others jealous of her. That Medea has acquired her (justifiably) evil reputation through this intelligence she as yet leaves unanswered.

The second part of her speech is a plea to Creon. She bears him no grudge and certainly has no ill feeling towards his family. She ends her defense with an appeal to let her remain in Corinth.

Creon's response is obstinate. Medea cannot stay in Corinth. He says that he is even more suspicious of her now.

A brief but rapid exchange follows in lines 325-344 in which Medea succeeds in changing Creon's mind. He is persuaded to delay her exile for a single day. Medea begs and abases herself in order to change Creon's mind. Medea also appeals to Creon's feelings towards his country and his family. *She* will have neither once she is exiled.

The debate ends with Medea successfully manipulating Creon into allowing her to remain in Corinth for a single extra day so that she can make arrangements for going into exile with her sons.

Creon relents and permits Medea to stay this extra day. The irony is that he knows that this is a foolish decision, but he agrees to it nonetheless;

*"You can hardly in one day accomplish*

*What I am afraid of"* (lines 355-356)

However, Creon consoles himself with the thought that Medea cannot possibly cause mischief in a single day. After this day she must go into exile on pain of death.

### Medea's Second *Rhesis* (lines 364-414)

Creon leaves and is not seen on stage again. He does not know it, but he has made a fatal error.

Medea is now alone on stage and addresses the Chorus and the audience.

Medea makes it clear that she has manipulated Creon. She has a clear plan and knows what she intends to do; she desires vengeance against Jason and Glauce and makes clear in this speech that she only begged Creon in order to change his mind. Medea has manipulated Creon through a show of tears and pleading in order to allow her to remain inn Corinth a single additional day.

In this day she will carry out her desire for revenge on Jason, Creon and Glauce, and she reveals that she will try to kill them.

In other Greek tragedies such as Euripides' *Hippolytus* and Sophocles' *Ajax,* a Goddess explains the fates in store for the eponymous protagonists. Here Euripides does the same. Medea explains to the audience the fate of Jason, Creon and Glauce and the reasons why. Euripides now has Medea embarking on a transformation; from wronged woman to avenging Goddess.

The decision has been made; Medea now needs to overcome a few more hurdles. She needs to decide upon how to kill her targets – should it be by setting their home on fire? Should it be by a sword as they sleep? She decides upon poison. Poison is an appropriate choice; it was often thought to be used by witches and sorceresses. Medea reveals also her origins and alludes to her divine nature in this speech. She is the daughter of a king and her Grandfather is no less than Helios – the Sun God. Medea then is revealed as a Demi-Goddess; not a normal woman and one it is probably best not to offend.

Another problem remains unsolved however. Medea does not yet know how she can escape unscathed after committing her murderous acts. She requires a place of refuge to escape to, but failing a place of refuge, she declares that she will still go through with the act and face the consequences. Medea then demonstrates that she is both courageous and determined and her own words provide a jaundiced view of women;

*"Useless for honest purposes,*

*But in all kinds of evil, skilled practitioners"* (Lines 412-413)

*Task: Medea*

*Write responses to the following;*

*Identify the language used by Euripides that demonstrates Medea's manipulative nature in this episode.*

*To what extent do you agree with the view that the fate of Creon, Jason and Glauce is sealed by this point of the play?*

**Exile in Ancient Greece**

A common punishment in Ancient Greece was to force an individual or group of people into exile. Individuals would also go into exile in order to avoid punishment.

Exile was often the punishment for those found guilty of homicide, but was also a good way for a polis to rid itself of an individual or group of people who were considered to be polluted.

In Athens in the 5th Century BC a form of temporary exile existed which was known as *ostracism*. *Ostracism* occurred when the Athenian citizen body voted for an *ostracism* (typically of someone in the political sphere). If over 6000 votes were cast, then the person with the most votes had to go into exile for a period of ten years.

However, unlike a regular exile, the ostracized individual remained an Athenian citizen, could be recalled at any time and had to remain relatively nearby. Their property and family were protected by the Athenian state and restored to the ostracized individual when they returned.

## 2.6: Exploring the Second Episode: Medea and Jason

This section will help you to;

- *Understand the mythical background of Jason.*

- *Explore the Second Episode of Medea.*

- *Understand and apply some key terminology.*

- *Consider the importance of the oikos in Greek Society.*

**Introduction**

In this second episode Euripides introduces a character who perhaps more than any other in this play deserves the description of a tragic hero; Jason.

In the Second Episode Jason tries to explain why he has abandoned Medea and married Glauce. Jason tries to explain that this is for the best, but fails to be convincing in this effort.

*Task: Jason*

*Read at the Second Episode again and consider the character of Jason;*

*Which of the following descriptions best describes the character of Jason in the second episode?*

- *a) That Jason is a reasonable and pragmatic man*
- *b) That Jason is cruel and arrogant*

**Jason in the Second Episode**

Jason is a hero and as such is concerned for his *timé* and *kleos*. But he is also ageing and an exile. He hopes to establish himself at Corinth and in order to do this he needs to both escape his past (for he was guilty of conspiracy to murder his Uncle Pelias in Iolcus) and he also needs to replace his non-Greek wife with another, more suitable bride if he is to fully integrate his *oikos* into the *polis* of Corinth.

Jason arrives onstage and immediately blames Medea's exile on her lack of *sophrosyne* (Self Control). Jason tries to counsel Medea and advises moderation. Jason claims that he will provide for Medea and the children when they are exiled.

Having arrived on stage and made his opening remarks, Euripides now has Medea and Jason engage in an *Agon* – a debate. This is the second *Agon* in the Medea (the first being that of Medea and Creon).

**Medea's *Rhesis* (lines 465-519)**

Medea is plainly furious with Jason in this episode. She insults Jason, calling him unmanly and a coward. Medea argues that she is the victim and has been cruelly mistreated by Jason. To support this, Medea gives the following evidence, taken from the myth of Medea, Jason and the quest for the Golden Fleece;

- Medea saved Jason's life when he had to plough a field with a team of fire breathing bulls.
- Medea killed the serpent that guarded the Golden Fleece.
- Medea abandoned her father and home in order to help Jason and the Argonauts escape.
- Medea killed King Pelias of Iolcus by deceiving his daughters.
- Medea married Jason and bore him sons.

Having established her previous assistance and loyalty to Jason, she now outlines her current predicament;

- She is unwelcome in Colchis, Iolcus and now Corinth.
- She has abandoned family and friends to be with Jason.
- She will be left to beg in the road once she is exiled.

Medea concludes her speech by again returning to disparaging Jason. She likens him and men to Pyrite (fool's gold) - if only men could bear identifying marks that could make it easy to tell the difference between good men and bad.

**Pelias about to be killed by his daughters**

**Jason's defense**

Medea's speech should in theory be a defense. Instead Euripides has reversed the order of the *Agon* and placed Medea's speech first. As such it is Medea who is the prosecution - accusing Jason.

Jason now responds. He likens his position to that of a ship facing a storm – a common enough metaphor. Jason counters that the Argonaut quest was completed because it had the blessing of Aphrodite. He acknowledges Medea's assistance but claims that Medea left a barbarian land in order to come with him to Greece. Since Greece is a land of order, civilization and justice, Jason has done Medea a favour, by bringing her with him. If Medea had not come to Greece, she would not be famous!

Jason then responds that his plan of marrying the princess Glauce is a wise and fortuitous act. He reminds her that they are both stateless exiles. By marrying Glauce, Jason will ensure the prosperity of his *oikos*, and this security will allow their sons to remain in Corinth in honour and in time perhaps become part of the elite of the city.

Jason then ends his defense with the misogynistic claim that Medea is jealous due to her female nature and passionate nature inherent in her sex. If children could be born without women; if women did not exist, then the world would be free of misery.

**Medea's response**

Medea replies that Jason is dishonest – why did he not speak to Medea about his plan to divorce her and marry Glauce first? Jason weakly tries to respond to this – it would not have helped as she would not listen. Medea then calls Jason an aging hero with an Asiatic wife. He is first and foremost concerned with his own reputation, as to have a foreign born wife was not respectable.

Jason tries to tell Medea that she is in fact a fortunate woman; if only she can see it. He can ensure the future of their children through this new marriage.

Medea now shifts discussion to her impending exile. Jason blames her for this also. She has slandered Creon publically and made him fear her. Jason then offers again to help Medea in her exile, but she refuses. Jason then leaves stage with Medea openly threatening his new marriage.

## The myth of Jason

Jason was a mythical Greek hero most famous for his quest to find and take the Golden Fleece; a magical ram's hide.

**Key terms:**

*timé – The pursuit of honour and esteem.*

*kleos – Good reputation.*

Jason was the son of Aeson and was born in Iolcus, a city in Thessaly. Aeson was king of Iolcus but was overthrown and killed by his brother Pelias (Jason's Uncle). Jason was according to myth raised by the wise Centaur Chiron in exile whilst Pelias ruled Iolcus.

Grown to adulthood, Jason returned to Iolcus and presented himself before Pelias, who agreed to surrender the kingship of Iolcus if Jason would undertake the quest to find and return with the Golden Fleece.

Jason gathered together a crew of heroes, including Heracles, and sailed to Colchis on a ship named *Argo*. After many trials and tribulations Jason and the Argonauts manage to take the Golden Fleece with the assistance of Medea, the daughter of the King of Colchis and also the divine help of the Goddesses Hera and Aphrodite.

The Argonaut quest was famous in antiquity and the *Argonautica* an epic poem of this quest was written in the 3$^{rd}$ Century BC by Apollonius of Rhodes. The epic poem *Argonautica* survives complete in four long books.

Jason and Medea return in triumph to Iolcus and are married. They present themselves to Pelias, who refuses to hand over the city to Jason. Pelias' daughters are deceived by Medea into killing their father in order to try and make him young again and Jason and Medea are forced into exile – travelling to Corinth; where Euripides' takes up this myth and the events that unfold in Corinth.

### The death of Jason

Jason dies in Greek myths in several ways.

According to some traditions Jason kills himself; in others he is crushed by the rotting timbers of the hull of the Argo as he sleeps underneath it, his home after he is forced out of Corinth due to the events in Euripides' *Medea*. Another tradition has Jason die when he is crushed by the stern piece of the Argo that was dedicated to the temple of Hera Acraea and placed in that temple when he attempted to enter this place in order to visit where his sons are buried by Medea.

### Medea and Jason

Jason is a character who provokes mixed reactions of dislike and sympathy. It is typical of Euripides that he presents us with men and women such as these, both likeable and unlikeable. We start the play for example by being presented with an arrogant Jason who abandons his wife. By the end of the play however, Euripides makes Jason a more sympathetic character; however, by the end of the play Jason has lost everything.

Although in some ways Jason stands for the civilised and ordered values that are desired in a stable and well organised Greek polis. Jason also represents the patriarchal male domination of the *polis*, and can be thought by many to be an arrogant, even unlikeable, character.

It is evident that Jason cares greatly about his children, but to modern readers he goes about this care in a remarkably unusual way. His decision to marry Glauce, the princess of Corinth, in order to ensure his status and in order to protect his oikos comes across to the modern reader as somewhat cold. Jason takes no account of how Medea or his children may feel about his decision.

### The importance of the *Oikos* to Greek Society

*Key terms:*

*Oikos – household*

*Kyrios – male head of the oikos*

Quite simply, we cannot overestimate the importance of the *oikos* in Ancient Greek society. The *oikos* was the household – the essential social, political and economic unit upon which the whole structure of Greek Society was built.

The *oikos* consisted typically of the father of the house, the mother of the house, their sons, daughters and slaves. The father was almost always the head of the household (*Kyrios*). If the father died however and he had an adult son, he would then become the *Kyrios*. In order of social importance the *oikos* hierarchy was essentially;

- Father
- Sons
- Mother
- Slaves/ Daughters

No *oikos* in Greek Society existed in isolation however; each oikos was linked to others in the *polis* (city state) through relatives and other familial connections. So these links included the married relatives, siblings, grandparents and so forth.

If the *Kyrios* of the oikos died, then it was possible for an uncle or brother to assume responsibility for the oikos, if no adult family members were left within the household.

## The *Oikos* in *Medea*: A defence of Jason's actions

The household in *Medea* is fairly typical at first; with Jason head of the house and includes Medea, their children and their *Oiketai* – or household slaves.

**Key term: Hamartia**

*Hamartia derives from a Greek root word meaning 'to miss the mark' or 'to fall short'. In the context of Greek tragedy, hamartia refers to a failing of the central character which brings about the catastrophe. It has sometimes been translated as a 'character flaw'; but this is to fall short of the true meaning of the word.*

*In fact, it is not so much an in-grained character fault as more an opportunity missed, or bad decision made which sets up the inescapability and inevitability of the tragic events which follow.*

However, Jason and Medea's *oikos* is unusual also because both Jason and Medea are foreigners in the city of Corinth; this means that their *oikos* exists in isolation in Corinth with no familial links to other Corinthian *oikoi*.

It is important to remember that whilst Medea is an exile from Colchis, it is easy to forget that Jason is also an exile – from Thessaly. Medea and Jason have no relatives in Corinth and therefore their position is that of outsiders and still highly vulnerable.

When we understand this position – we can also therefore understand some justification for Jason's actions. He needs to make connections in Corinth both for himself and his family. Since his children are far too young, he cannot marry them into the *oikos* of another family in Corinth for many more years.

Jason exists in Corinth largely on sufferance of his great reputation and honour as a hero (his *timé* and *kleos*). But the quest of the Argonauts ended some years ago and over time his *timé* and *kleos* will fall into decline unless he continues to maintain it. He has already been forced into exile through the actions of Medea against his Uncle Pelias and so he has arrived in Corinth with his *oikos* under something other than ideal circumstances.

When Jason manages to persuade Creon to give him the hand of his daughter Glauce in marriage, Jason then is given the opportunity in order to both preserve his heroic reputation and, more importantly, provide links to safeguard his *oikos* in the wider community of Corinth.

Jason however must divorce Medea in order to marry Glauce Although this is tough for her, Jason is acting to build and protect his *oikos*, of which Medea is a replaceable member. This reasonable logic however overlooks a crucial flaw in the plan; Medea is not a normal Ancient Greek woman. She is a dangerous demi-Goddess with a proven track record of violence and has not hesitated in the past to kill even her own brother if it means she can ensure her own self-preservation.

*Task: Jason and his oikos*

*Write a response to the following question;*

*To what extent do you agree with the view that Jason's primary concern is for the wellbeing of his oikos?*

*Task: Hamartia*

*Write a response to the following question;*

*To what extent do you agree with the view that the hamartia of the play principally occurs in the Second Episode?*

## 2.7: Exploring the Third Episode: Medea and Aegeus

This section will help you to;

- *Explore and understand Episode Three.*

- *Understand the role of Aegeus in the play.*

- *Explore and understand a Rhesis.*

- *Consider the silence of the Nurse in this episode.*

### Introduction

In the Third Episode of Euripides' *Medea* the tone of the play shifts slightly. Previously Medea has been faced by opposition in the form of Creon and Jason. Now however, Medea encounters a would be if unwitting ally; Aegeus.

Aegeus will give Medea the sanctuary required in order for her plan to succeed.

### Who was Aegeus?

Aegeus was a mythical king of Athens and a possible father of the more famous Theseus.

Aegeus was one of the ten Attic heroes who gave his name to one of the ten tribes of Attica, which formed part of the Social organisational blocks of Athenian society.

In myth Aegeus was known for being childless. In despair at this position, Aegeus consulted the Delphic oracle and was ordered to abstain from sex until he returned to Athens. On his return to Athens, Aegeus' wife, Aethra had a child shortly after; the Hero Theseus. However in other myths Theseus' father was the god Poseidon.

Aegeus is also known in myth for marrying Medea after she had been abandoned by Jason. Once in Athens Medea attempted to poison Theseus, but failed in this and was exiled by Aegeus.

Aegeus also sent his son Theseus to Crete. Theseus confronted and killed the Minotaur in Crete and on his return to Athens forgot to raise a white sail to indicate that he had succeeded in killing the

Minotaur. Failing to see this signal and believing that Theseus was dead; Aegeus in grief threw himself off the cliffs and died.

## Aegeus' oracle

Medea is not entirely without friends and allies in Greece however. Aegeus is the King of Athens and has come to Corinth. Aegeus has his own problems and hopes that Medea can advise him.

Aegeus has been to Delphi in order to consult the oracle of Apollo. He is now travelling to visit his friend the king of Troezon and since Corinth is on the way, this explains why Aegeus is here.

Aegeus is childless and has questioned the oracle on how to rectify this. He has been given a cryptic response and hopes that Medea understands Apollo's instruction;

*"He commanded me 'not to unstop the wineskin's neck'.*

(Line 705)

The command is to avoid having sex until Aegeus has returned to Athens. In the fifth Century the father of Theseus (the idealised hero of Athens) was either Aegeus or Poseidon. In a later play (*Hippolytus*) Euripides has Theseus' father as the god Poseidon therefore if Euripides' consistently believed that Theseus was the son of Poseidon and not Aegeus; then this cryptic response of the Delphic Oracle was superfluous. However, in the myths associated with Medea, it is Medea who helps Aegeus conceive a child through the application of her drugs and magic.

*Task: The character of Medea in Episode Three*

*Write a response to the following question;*

*What does this episode tell us about Medea's character?*

### Medea and Aegeus

Aegeus now asks what is wrong with Medea. She explains that Jason has left her for Glauce and that she now faces exile. Medea appeals to Aegeus as a supplicant; let her come to Athens and live there after she is exiled from Corinth. Medea offers her services as a sorceress; she will use her drugs and knowledge in order to make Aegeus fertile. Unlike her earlier conversations with men, Medea is genuine in her request. She needs Aegeus' help and Athens as a place of refuge. However, she is still manipulative; she offers her services and knowledge in order to give Aegeus extra incentive to accept her request.

Aegeus agrees and needs little persuasion. But he does state that Medea must travel to Athens herself. He does not want to take her with him and risk offending the Corinthians.

Medea accepts, but she is sceptical of men. She wants a guarantee that Aegeus will not in future turn her over to her enemies in Iolcus or in Corinth. Aegeus does not choose to inquire too closely as to why the Corinthians or Iolchians should want to pursue Medea. Instead Aegeus naively accepts and offers to swear to whichever Gods Medea chooses.

Medea asks Aegeus to swear to all Gods, but especially the Earth and the Sun – this selection is notable as although the Greeks acknowledged that the Earth and the Sun were indeed Gods, they were more typically worshipped by barbarian foreigners. Aegeus swears nonetheless, never to expel Medea from Attica.

### Medea's Speech (lines 766-829)

Aegeus leaves the stage and Medea is left alone on stage only with the Chorus and the Nurse, who remains silent.

Medea now exults that a major obstacle to success in her plan has been overcome. Previously Medea had been willing to take revenge, but not being able to escape feared that she would be killed after carrying out her revenge. Now she can escape.

Euripides now has Medea explain to the Chorus, the Nurse and the audience what her plan will be.

Medea will summon Jason and manipulate him into believing that she has changed her mind and now approves of his marriage to Glauce. Medea will beg that Jason takes the children to Glauce with gifts for the princess. These gifts will be poisoned and will kill Glauce. The Euripides has Medea announce another major reveal; she will kill her children.

The only response to Medea comes from the Chorus. They urge Medea not to do carry out this dreadful plan. Medea however ignores the Chorus and sends the Nurse off to Jason with instructions to summon him. The Nurse is ordered to silence.

---

**Task: The Nurse**

*Write a response to the following question;*

*Why do you think the Nurse is silent in this episode?*

*Given her dialogue in the prologue she is very protective of the children – yet here she obeys willingly, without comment.*

*Do you think that Euripides adequately explains the reasoning for Nurse's non-action is that she is?*

*"a loyal servant, And a woman..." Lines 828-829*

---

## 2.8: Exploring the Fourth Episode: Medea manipulates Jason

This section will help you to;

- Explore the characters of Jason and Medea in this part of the play.

- Begin to explore the themes of Manipulation and Synome (Forgiveness) in Euripides' Medea.

- Consider the gifts as a plot device.

**Jason and Medea Part Two.**

The Fourth Episode of Medea is just over one hundred lines of the play; however it is a key part of the play. In the Fourth Episode Medea manipulates Jason into taking the children to visit Glauce, loaded down with her poisonous gifts.

**Medea manipulates Jason**

Medea has sent for Jason and now he duly arrives. He asks what she wants. Medea asks Jason to forgive her earlier words and rage. Medea says that she has acted like a fool and her behaviour in the Second Episode was wrong. Medea admits that she was not listening to the advice that others were giving her and she did not realise that other people; the Chorus and Jason himself were just trying to help her.

Medea now declares that she sees that the children will be cared for by Glauce and in time they will perhaps become the brothers of royalty. She thanks Jason for making this alliance with the royal house of Corinth and states that Jason was right and that she Medea was wrong.

This of course is all an act. Medea has not changed her mind at all, as the audience well knows. Medea has not forgiven Jason for abandoning her and her speech is solely designed to ensure that Jason is manipulated into doing what Medea wants; to deliver the children to Glauce so they can give her the poisoned gifts.

Medea however goes further. She not only is manipulating Jason, but she is also manipulating their children. She calls the children out onto stage (accompanied by the Tutor) and she begs them to embrace their father – their quarrel is ended and the family are all reconciled once more.

However, this manipulation comes at a cost to Medea. She begins to weep at the thought of losing her children;

*Forgive me; I recalled*

*What pain the future hides from us".*

Medea (Lines 900-901)

This reveals a more humane character to Medea. She is upset by the thought of losing her children; but not to the point that she cannot bear to go through with her vengeance, which is a much stronger element that dominates her character.

---

**Task: The character of Medea in Episode Four**

*Write a response to the following question;*

*To what extent do you agree with the view that Medea's tears are, like the rest of her words and actions in Episode Four, no more than an act?*

---

### The naivety of Jason?

Jason too is consolatory in this episode. However the difference between his and Medea's words however are that they are genuine, if misguided, as well as misogynistic.

Jason states that he understands her resentment against him and Glauce, but that Medea has now arrived at the right decision. Jason states that their children will be in time leading men of Corinth. The irony here is clearly apparent;

*'Only grow big and strong...'*

(Lines 918-920)

These final lines of Jason here draw out more tears from Medea. He notices and asks why she is upset at his words. Even now, Jason cannot see that Medea has more on her mind than simple grief at being parted from her children.

Medea wonders whether the children will grow up. She urges Jason to persuade Creon to let them stay. Jason is uncertain, so Medea now asks him to take the children to Glauce; she will be able to persuade her father surely?

### The role of the Chorus in Episode Four

The Chorus play the role of the hapless onlookers in this episode. They realise that the children are in danger from Medea's plot, but are unable through the convention of Greek tragedy to intervene in the events unfolding before them. In this, the Chorus are representative of the audience; witnessing events, but being powerless to intervene.

### The poisoned gifts

Jason agrees and Medea then proceeds with her plan. She has gifts for Glauce; a coronet and a dress that she has already selected. But when did Medea select these gifts? She has not left the stage since before her conversation with Creon. There are then two explanations for this;

- Medea has already planned for this eventuality and prepared her poisonous gifts before she was exiled by Creon.
- Euripides has not carefully accounted for this plot hole and it is a flaw in the composition of the play.

If it is the first then Medea has been directing the events of the play all along and known in advance what the ultimate outcome will be.

These gifts are brought forth by a maid and carried by the children in a casket. Jason is curious about these gifts and queries why Medea would let such fantastic treasures leave her possession. Jason still does not realise that there is a plot afoot. He tries to claim that Glauce's regard for himself should be sufficient to persuade her to look after the children. Medea though even takes this away from Jason; mortals are after all more persuaded by gifts than by arguments.

Medea's final words are leading and addressed to her children;

*"Go quickly; be successful, and bring good news back,*

*That what your mother longs for has been granted you".*

(Lines 973-974)

Medea's final words are more like a general sending a warrior into battle than those of a mother saying farewell to her children possibly for the last time. She is even perhaps envious that it is the children that will deliver the vengeance that she desires and not her.

---

**Task: Episode Four**

*Write a response to the following question;*

> *"Jason could prevent the tragedy in Episode Four if he refused to take his children to visit Glauce".*

> *To what extent do you agree with this view?*

---

**Task: The character of Jason in Episode Four**

*In the Second Episode we considered the character of Jason with the following question;*

*Which of the following descriptions best describes the character of Jason in the second episode?*

> a) *That Jason is a reasonable and pragmatic man*
> b) *That Jason is cruel and arrogant*

*Has your view of Jason changed at all by Episode Four?*

## 2.9: Exploring the Fifth Episode: Medea and her children

This section will help you to;

- Explore the fifth episode.

- Consider the reversal of fortune and dramatic irony in Medea.

- Understand the role and function of the kommos in Medea.

- Consider the role of children in Greek Society.

**Introduction**

The Fifth episode is a short one, consisting of just under eighty lines and involves two speaking characters; the Tutor and Medea, and two non-speaking characters; the children. It is in this episode that Medea resolves to kill her children.

**The Tutor's news and reception by Medea**

The Tutor enters the stage with the children in tow. He is bringing good news to Medea and cannot wait to tell her; the Children are no longer banished. Glauce has accepted the gifts and the children are no longer in any danger.

If Medea was a normal mother she would be happy that her children are no longer in danger and could console herself that, even though she is to go into exile, her children will be safe with their father.

However, Medea is not a normal mother. She is instead saddened by this news and her response comes as a surprise to the Tutor. He does not know that Medea has sent poisoned gifts to Glauce and that her children are now polluted through their association with her crime.

The children now have to die, but Medea will have to kill them in the knowledge that she could have kept them out of her quest for revenge. If Medea had gone into exile without taking revenge, in time she could have been reunited with her children. Now, of course, this is too late.

The irony of this situation is compounded by Tutor's lack of understanding and Medea's reply;

T: *"Take heart, mistress; in time your sons will bring you home".*

**Key term: Kommos**

M: *"Before then, I have others to send home. Oh, Gods!"*

*A Kommos is a lament. Often a kommos is a lyrical exchange between the Chorus and a character, but can also be a monologue.*

The Tutor means that the children will in time be able to bring Medea home to them once they are grown. Medea however has a different meaning for the word 'home'; she means that she has others still to kill; her children.

**Task: The Kommos**

*Explore the emotive language used by Euripides in this kommos.*

*To what extent do you think Medea truly regrets her decision or is it all for show?*

### Medea's *kommos*

Medea's *kommos* is one of the highlights of the play. In the *kommos* Euripides uses his innovative skill to have Medea address both the children and the chorus, as she laments the situation she finds herself in, that she herself has caused.

At first Medea addresses the children. The Children now have a home, but she must go into exile and never see them growing up or see them marry. Now, however, Medea sees the effort she has invested in raising them as futile; it is they who should bury her, but the reverse will be true now.

Having addressed the children, Medea now addresses the Chorus. Here she weakens in her resolve. She will escape, but she will now take the children with her. However, this wavering only lasts for a short time; the children must die in order for her to inflict the most pain on her enemy Jason.

Medea then requests of the Chorus (and by extension the audience) she requests that all who lack the strength to witness her revenge, her sacrifice, leave now. As the children start to head indoors, Medea says farewell to her children. She is sad certainly, but has now hardened herself and is determined to kill her own children.

**Medea murdering one of her children**

### Children in Ancient Greece

Medea's children enter the stage again in the fifth episode. They have been exercising – which is part of the education of young children in Athens. In this they have been overseen by the character known as Tutor.

### The uncertainty of childhood in Ancient Greece

In Ancient Greece the father of a child decided once the child was born whether or not the new-born would live or die. If the decision was made to kill a child, the child would be taken out into the countryside and exposed to the elements.

This may sound barbaric to us today but a child may have been exposed for many reasons; perhaps the family could not afford to feed and raise the child, perhaps the family already had a number of children and in the Ancient World contraception was at best primitive and probably mostly ineffective. In this case exposure was a form of birth control.

Perhaps the child had some physical disabilities. In the Ancient World, a lack of medical knowledge and medicines would make it often very likely that a new-born with physical disabilities would be unlikely to survive to adulthood.

Children were officially recognised by their family after five days in a ceremony called the 'amphidromia' which recognised that the family now had a new member. Mortality rates in Ancient Greek families were however high and a baby might not survive beyond their first few years.

At around the age of six, children spent much of their time being cared by their mothers, or nurses if the family was wealthy enough to be able to afford a slave to undertake these duties. The father would not really have much role in raising children until they were older.

## Education in Ancient Athens

The Tutor in Medea, is known in Greek as a *'Paedagógus'*, literally a 'Child leader', and he, like the Nurse, is a slave. A Tutor was employed by the family to raise children and to maintain order and discipline of the children whilst they were aged between seven and fourteen.

As mentioned above, the children enter on stage in the Fifth Episode, having returned from running. Running and physical education were an integral part of the education of young children in Ancient Athens. At Athens children were trained in physical education by a *'Paidotribes'*; either a private or state owned slave that taught physical education and athletics. This education would often take place at the *palaestra* – a publically owned wrestling and exercise ground.

Other teachers would teach reading and writing and also music was commonly taught until the age of fourteen. After this age some children would continue in education, but for most, their education would end around this age and they would begin to work full time.

**Key term: Paedagógus**

*Literally; a 'Child Leader'.*

*A slave responsible for the education and discipline of children.*

## 2.10: The Sixth Episode: Medea and the Messenger

This section will help you to;

• *Understand the role and function of the Messenger Speech.*

• *Consider the reversal of fortune in Medea.*

• *Explore the language used in the Messenger Speech.*

• *Consider Medea's reaction to the Messenger Speech.*

**Introduction**

In this section we will explore the Messenger Speech. The Messenger Speech is one of the most effective and common devices that can be used by Greek Tragedians.

*Key term: Messenger Speech*

*In contrast to the reasoned argument characteristic of the Rhesis or the Agon, the Messenger Speech makes full use of appeal to the audience's emotions. These speeches are used as a reporting device of the tragedians, and allowed them to describe the violence vividly, a consequence of their characters' actions, without breaking the taboo of representing violence on-stage. The messenger speeches take the form of narrative; a messenger arrives to report on what he has seen take place out of sight of the audience.*

*Task: Analysing the language of the Messenger Speech*

*Explore the language of the Messenger Speech.*

*What aspects might an audience find shocking and or entertaining in this speech?*

### The reception of the Messenger Speech: A reversal of convention

Euripides however uses the Messenger Speech in a somewhat different way in the *Medea*. Typically the Messenger's Speech brings news of disaster to a character on stage, who then realises the consequences of an action or event.

What Euripides does in this Messenger Speech **is to bring good news to Medea.** The content of the Messenger Speech is still full of horror and calamity, but the reception of the news by Medea is the opposite of what is normal. As in other places in *Medea*, Euripides has reversed the traditional convention.

*Task: Analysing the reaction to the children*

*What is the reaction of the Servants to the children in the Messenger Speech?*

*How does this compare with Glauce's reaction to them?*

*How effective do you think Euripides' language is in illustrating these reactions?*

### The Messenger Speech

The Messenger enters stage calling on Medea to flee. She has committed a terrible crime; she has killed both Glauce and Creon.

Medea's reaction is a combination of calmness and joy *'Your news is excellent'*. The comparison of the characters on stage is interesting. Medea is calm and happy, whereas the Messenger is in a state of shock.

The Messenger replies that Medea must be mad to have acted in such a way against the royal house of Corinth. The Messenger now tells his story.

Jason and the Children enter the palace and go to see Glauce. The Servants are pleased by their arrival and welcome them. The Princess however seems to want to ignore them initially. It is only when Jason insists that she acknowledges them. Jason and the children now depart the palace.

---

**Task: Analysing the language of death**

Consider the death scenes of Glauce and Creon.

How effective do you think Euripides' language is in illustrating these deaths?

---

Glauce is happy to receive the gifts and puts on the coronet and the dress. Euripides now demonstrates Glauce's pleasure at the gifts, he has the princess look at herself in the mirror and dance around her room in them.

Then the poison takes effect. Glauce slumps into a chair and begins to shake. Possibly her symptoms resemble an epileptic seizure, as an attending servant mistakes the sudden reaction of Glauce as the anger of Pan and begins to sing a song of worship to help avert the seizure. The attendant maid then realises that the affliction of the princess is something more and suspects poison. She calls for Jason to return.

What happens next is both graphic and disturbing. Glauce wakens but immediately starts to be burned by the coronet on her head. It is so tight fitting that it will not come off. The dress meanwhile secretes a different kind of poison and begins to eat her flesh.

Glauce is no longer dancing around the room. But she runs about in pain and suffering trying futilely to remove the cursed items. Eventually she is overcome and collapses to the ground; a burned and melted corpse; barely recognizable.

Euripides' uses a graphic simile to illustrate Glauce's painful demise;

*"Attacked by the invisible fangs of poison, melted*

*From the bare bone, like gum-drops from a pine-trees' bark".*

*(Lines 1198-1199)*

Creon now enters the Messenger Speech. He sees what is left of his beloved daughter on the floor and rushes to embrace her. The dress that has melted Glauce is still potent and begins to melt Creon too.

---

**Take Note!**

**Off Stage Action**

The Deaths of Glauce and Creon can be graphic and brutally described by Euripides in such a way that would be impossible to replicate on stage.

The power of imagination is much more sophisticated than any acting or special effect than the Ancient playwright could hope to perform on stage.

Euripides uses almost Homeric language to describe the death of Creon;

*"Weakened with pain, he yielded and gasped out his life"*

(Line 1220)

The Messenger now brings his speech to an end with the final pessimistic lines that human life is but a shadow; that those who are the most intelligent are the guiltiest of folly and that happiness is for mortals an unobtainable goal.

The Messenger now departs the stage and Medea is left alone with the Chorus, who interject that calamity has struck a blow on Jason. This blow Medea now intends to make heavier.

Medea now must carry out the part of the plan which she is more conflicted with; the murder of her own children in order to cause Jason the most possible pain.

The Children's fate is now sealed. Medea expresses some doubts however and seeks to justify her actions.

If she delays in killing the children or hesitates then the Corinthians will be certain to kill them. Medea steals herself to prepare for the act, but her final words of her monologue are selfish;

*"Life has been cruel to me"*

(Line 1251)

---

**Task: Conventions and Euripides**

Write a response to the following question;

*Euripides breaks some conventions and sticks with others. To what extent does the play Medea provide evidence to support this view?*

---

## 2.11: Exodus: Medea triumphant

This section will help you to;

- *Explore the end of the play.*

- *Explore the characters of Jason and Medea in the exodus.*

- *Understand some key terms of Greek Tragedy.*

- *Consider whether the ancient audience would find the end of the play satisfying.*

### Introduction

The final scene of the play has now arrived. Medea has carried out her murder of Glauce and Creon and has taken the irrevocable step of killing her children in cold blood. This death has been carried out off-stage (according to tragic tradition) and the chorus have been powerless to intervene (again, in line with tragic convention).

### The Exodus

**Key term:**
**Anagnorisis**

Recognition.

A change from ignorance to awareness of a bond of love or hate.

Jason comes running onto stage, fearful and enraged. All his former calmness and rational demeanour of has now vanished. He has run from the palace, having learned of the dreadful fate of Glauce and Creon.

Jason blusters that Medea will be punished for the murder of Glauce and Creon, but he is at the moment most in fear for the safety of his children. He fears that the Corinthians will take their revenge out on the boys. Jason questions the chorus and is told to expect bad news. It is interesting to note that Jason's first reaction is to ask whether Medea intends to kill *him*. Even now he has not considered that Medea would kill her own flesh and blood.

> **Task: The Exodus**
>
> How effective do you find the end of the play?
>
> What do you think are the most satisfying elements?
>
> What are the least?

**Medea aloft in the chariot of Helios**

**Medea's Chariot**

The Chorus reveal the terrible news that Medea has killed the children. As Jason fails to batter the doors of Medea's house down, Medea appears on the roof of the *skene* in the chariot of the Sun God. Drawn by dragons Medea also has the bodies of the slain children clearly visible.

The transformation of Medea is now complete; from a grief-stricken woman at the beginning of the play, Medea is now transfigured into a divine-being, borne into the skies by the chariot of her grandfather, Helios, the Sun-God. Medea is now untouchable and removed from the justice that any mortal can hope to mete out to her.

This depiction of Medea in a chariot would no doubt have been the set piece to the finale of the play. Euripides would want the departure of Medea to be as exciting as possible for his audience.

---

**Jason's *Anagnorisis***

Jason is now full of regret. He regrets bringing a foreign woman with him to Corinth. Gone is his calmness and reserve. He is now distraught and enraged – much like Medea was in the early stages of the play; the reversal of the characters is now complete.

However, Jason largely has himself to blame. He brought Medea to Greece in full knowledge of what she was like;

- Jason knew that Medea was a Sorceress
- Jason knew that Medea was a Demi-Goddess
- Jason knew that Medea was capable of murder
- Jason knew that Medea had abandoned her family

Jason is reduced to name-calling only. He calls Medea a polluted murderess, but that is all he can do. He begins to grieve for his sons and his slaughtered bride.

Medea replies that Jason dishonoured her and brought all this grief upon himself. Glauce was likewise wrong in presuming to try to replace *her*, and Creon was also in the wrong to exile her.

Jason retorts that the murder of children is Medea's loss also. Medea agrees with this, but states that she is justified in this murder simply to cause Jason the most pain possible.

**Key term: Katharsis**

*Katharsis gives us our word 'cathartic' which we use to refer to something with a great cleansing or purging power.*

*The word in the context of Greek tragedy refers to the effect a 'good' tragedy should have on the audience. It should purge the audience of its emotions, by inducing feelings such as pity, anger or fear and allowing the audience a safe place for the expression of them*

Both continue to blame each other, and Jason appeals to Medea to give up the corpses of his children so that he can bury them. Medea refuses. She will bury them in the temple of Hera Acraea (on the Corinthian Acropolis). She then pronounces their respective fates; Medea is to go to Athens, whilst Jason will age and die under the fallen timbers of his old ship the *Argo*.

Jason is broken. He cannot avenge himself on Medea, he cannot get his dead children back, and he now faces an uncertain future in Corinth.

The play ends with Medea travelling off in her chariot and Jason is left alone with his grief.

---

### Task: Katharsis?

Write responses to the following questions;

a) To what extent do you think the play achieves the aim of providing *Katharsis* for the audience?

b) To what extent is anyone entirely innocent in Euripides' *Medea*?

Consider the following characters;
- Medea
- Jason
- Glauce
- Creon
- Aegeus
- Children

---

**PART THREE:**

Themes in Euripides' *Medea*

## 3.1: Medea: foreign, female and fear of the 'Other'

In this topic we will;

- *Consider why the Greeks were suspicious of foreigners and women.*

- *Explore the Character of Medea.*

- *Consider the idea that Euripides sought to teach his audience.*

### Medea; *foreign and female*

To a Greek audience who that drew a sharp distinction between 'Greek' and 'barbarian' (that is, any non-Greek speaker) the defining characteristic of Medea is that she is foreign. Medea comes from a place called Colchis, far away on the shores of the Black Sea and from within the sphere of influence of the Persian Empire.

Medea then is *different* from the start: she is exotic and has magical powers. The modern viewer can therefore feel some sympathy for her as the eternal outsider, but the knowledge of her actions from before the start of the play should make us wary of Medea. Here is a woman capable of killing her own brother in order to evade capture by her father, and it was also she who killed King Pelias by manipulating and fooling his daughters.

Clearly, Medea then is no stranger to the murder of powerful people or close family members, and as such she is a woman of extremes; Medea's emotions swing from between the powerful love she feels for her two sons and powerful and overwhelming hatred she has for Jason, whom she despises for having destroyed her *timé* (honour) and her *kleos* (reputation) by his abandonment of her and their sons.

Athenian thought and society was preoccupied with various dichotomies which were held to be strict and controlling definitions.

- Male/Female.
- Greek/Barbarian.

To the Ancient Athenians then, there was a clear distinction between the codes of behaviour and separate spheres of influence appropriate to men and women, as there was a clear line between Greeks (usually defined as those who speak a recognisable form of Greek) and non-Greek speakers, or barbarians.

Foreigners and outsiders in Greek society suffered from this discrimination, and could find themselves scapegoats and objects of suspicion. The perceptions of the Ancient Athenians of outsiders and foreigners were inevitably coloured by this discrimination, since non-Greek speakers also stood for what has been termed *'the other'*, that is, for whatever which is unlike oneself and so as a consequence is to be feared, hated, mistrusted and shunned.

The Athenians had some grounds to be suspicious and mistrustful of foreigners. In 480BC their city was burned and destroyed by the Persian armies of Xerxes. The Persians destroyed not only the homes and businesses of the Athenians, but also desecrated the temples and sacred spaces of the Athenians. For decades afterwards the Athenians had led a coalition of Greek cities in a war aimed at both preserving the independence of Greece from Persia, but also to avenge themselves for this destruction of the city.

Often, the Ancient Greeks considered themselves to represent civilisation, or ordered values, in an otherwise chaotic universe where the rule of the barbarian, or chaos, could be seen everywhere else. It therefore matters a great deal to the Athenian audience that Medea is a foreigner, since as a foreigner she more or less automatically stands for disorder and chaos (this view is enhanced even more so when we include that Medea is a woman who possesses magical powers) and Medea's *'foreignness'* would certainly have been of importance for the original audience of this play.

Just as foreigners or outsiders were *'the other'* in the Athenian mind, so were women. Thus, men stood for the forces of order against the forces of chaos which women seemed to represent. On the other hand, the Ancient Athenians considered women to be irrational, uncontrollable and unpredictable. Women, if not controlled, had the power to bring down the order of the *oikos* and the *polis*, and with it the civilised and ordered values that the Athenians cherished. Because women were seen as socially and morally inferior to men, they were also therefore a potential threat to the order of society and if they were not controlled this reflected badly upon the males responsible for them.

Therefore, Medea as a foreigner *and* a woman is a representative of two forms of *'otherness'*, an entity to be feared.

### Sophistic reasoning in *Medea*

Euripides has clearly been influenced by sophistic reasoning in his writing, and he enjoys working in examples of this in both Medea's and Jason's speeches in this play. Both characters make use of sophistic reasoning at various points; Jason to justify his abandonment of Medea and his second marriage, Medea to justify murder of her children.

For example:

*Medea*, lines 522-543: '*I have to show myself a clever speaker ... and that's my answer*'. This is part of the set debate, or *agon*, between Jason and Medea.

Jason starts his answer with an interesting sea-faring metaphor. He says '*I'll furl all but an inch/ Of sail, and ride it out*'. This image is indicative of his general character. He is a self-composed and self-possessed man who prides himself on not reaching to excesses in any matter. The image here, of careful navigational control, bears this out.

Jason finds Medea's extreme emotions distasteful, and is seemingly unaware of the havoc that he has wreaked on Medea's self-worth. In this, he is self-possessed and controlled to the point of coldness. His *hamartia* (fatal flaw or mistake) is to fail to appreciate the consequences of his actions on the feelings of others. Jason is too self-absorbed and considerate only of his own position only; Medea's impassioned pleas and arguments fail to move him in this episode.

Jason dismisses any notion of Medea's help for Jason in the past in the remainder of this section. Instead, he credits Aphrodite for success in retrieving the Golden Fleece. Patronizingly, he says '*I admit, you have intelligence*' but he scorns what he considers is Medea's 'helpless passion' even though without her, Jason certainly would not have been successful in his quest to obtain the Golden Fleece.

Although Jason's logic leaves much to be desired, since he dismisses much of Medea's former help; Jason's speech is highly effective at further enraging Medea. Jason could be seen to be exulting in the power and authority he holds over Medea. Jason almost sees himself as emancipated and liberated from Medea. He has the freedom he has to marry who he wishes, while at the same time enjoying the fact that for Medea who is a foreign woman in Greek society, she has little or no power compared to that which she possessed during the quest for the Fleece.

### Euripides the teacher

The contemporary view of the tragedian as a socially engaged 'teacher' fits with Euripides' fondness for making mythical-heroic characters speak in ways which clearly draw on the social experiences of the fifth-century Athenian audience. When Medea speaks of the unhappy situation of mature married women, brought to what is for her, a foreign land she speaks as a barbarian yet, much of what Medea says shows a remarkable empathy with what must have been the lot of many Athenian wives.

Whether there were women in the tragic audience of the *City Dionysia* or not, Medea's words also speak directly and powerfully to Athenian men. Of course, there is also much about Medea that would allow an Athenian male to disassociate her from the real women in his life: there is her self-portrayal as a Homeric warrior seeking respect and revenge in a manner worthy of Achilles. There is also her manifest barbarity and her divine origins.

But Medea's famous speech at the end of the first episode connects her extreme response to Jason's faithlessness to recognizable Athenian social reality. Medea oscillates between two positions throughout this speech. Medea is sympathetic in terms that might make Athenian men think carefully about their responsibilities as husbands. But, as the play progresses towards the shocking climax of the infanticide and exodus Medea can also be viewed as a negative paradigm against which one can contrast Athenian ideals of womanhood.

*Task: Medea the Other*

*Write a response to the following question;*

*What would be more disturbing to an Ancient Audience that saw this play – That Medea is a foreigner or that Medea is a Woman?*

## 3.2: The role of the Chorus in *Medea*

In this topic we will;

- *Consider the role of the Chorus in Medea.*

- *Explore the Choral Odes of Medea.*

### Introduction

This topic focuses more closely on the role of the Chorus. In many Greek Tragedies the Chorus has an extended and important role to play. This is not the case however in Euripides' *Medea*. In this topic we shall examine the Choral Odes (*stasimon*) of *Medea*

### The Chorus

The Chorus in *Medea* are represented as Corinthian Women; they are women who appear to be friends with Medea.

As is typical in Greek tragedy the Chorus are not present on stage at the commencement of the play. They enter after the Nurse and Tutor have introduced the outline the plot in the *prologue*. The Chorus often enter the stage singing. However, as we have seen, the *parados* is interrupted by both the Nurse and by Medea offstage. Rather than a song, the Chorus are asking questions about the state of Medea.

Choral figures dancing on the Attic Red Figure Column Krater; 'the 'basel dancer'

**Task: Interpreting a red figure column krater**

*One valuable source we have for the Greek theatre is how it is depicted on pottery.*

*Evaluate how useful this pot is as a source of information about the Chorus in Greek tragedy.*

*What information does this red figure column krater provide?*

**Choral songs compared to dialogue between individuals in *Medea***

The Chorus is an effective tool used by the tragic playwrights. The Chorus can voice the fears and anxiety of the spectators to an event whose outcome is unknown. Unlike dialogue between characters or the monologues delivered by individual characters, choral songs differ in significant ways. Whilst monologues or dialogue between characters are usually quite clear, choral songs can often be difficult to understand for modern readers.

Some Choral songs in *Medea* feature mythical allusions which help the audience to understand the play; others are prayers to the gods and references to the situation on stage. In this, the Chorus of *Medea* is fulfilling its traditional function and role, as is seen in other Greek tragedies.

In Euripides' *Electra*, for example, the Chorus is consistently loyal to Electra; however, the Chorus in *Medea* veers in their sympathy. They begin as sympathetic to Medea and her plight. However by the end of the play the Chorus has shifted their sympathy to Jason.

Unlike in other plays however, the Chorus leader in *Medea* does not interact directly with the main characters in any detail. Unlike Sophocles, who keeps his Odes fairly uniform in structure in plays such as *Antigone*, Euripides' plays with the structure of the Choral Odes (*Stasimon*)

Some Odes have four verses, two *strophes* and two *antistrophe*, mostly similar in length but often the epode is missing entirely. The epode is a final verse or a section that brings the focus of the audience back to the action onstage.

---

### Key Term: Stasimon

*Stasimon* – A structured Choral Ode sung with dancing. It bought together themes from the preceding section of the play and explores the moral issues involved.

### The first *Choral Ode after the Parados - First stasimon* (lines 414-446)

There are two verses of reasonable duration (*Strophé* and *Antistrophé*) in this *stasimon,* with no *epode.*

The subject of the first verse is the reversal of the natural order of things. Females shall be honoured, deceit is a device of men and men's oaths are a sign of god's dishonour.

The subject of the second verse is the plight of Medea. Medea is alone, in exile and a stranger in a foreign land; abandoned by her husband and forsaken by her father.

There is a warning in this Choral Ode. Balance and a woman's place are precarious. There is a warning in this Stasimon that could at this stage apply to both Medea and the audience. This *stasimon* therefore is a foreshadowing of future events in *Medea.*

### The second *stasimon* (lines 628-662)

The second *stasimon* has four verses (Two *Strophés* and Two *Antistrophés*) in this *stasimon* with no *epode.*

The first pair of verses consists of a prayer to Aphrodite. The first is a prayer to the gentle Goddess of love Aphrodite, the second is a prayer to a different aspect of the Goddess – the Cyprian alludes to the passionate, wild aspect of love's desire. Not even the gods can resist this kind of love. It causes havoc and madness everywhere it turns.

The next pair of verses relate to the plight of Medea. She is to be exiled. Exile in the Ancient World was feared punishment issued to those guilty of pollution of crimes such as homicide.

### The third *stasimon* (Lines 830-867)

Again, this Choral Ode comprises of four verses, but again, there is no *epode.*

The first pair of verses is a song in praise of Athens, and Aphrodite's love of the city of Athens.

However, in the third verse the Chorus shift the tone of the song and instead sing of the threat that Medea presents to the city of Athens. How will they welcome a polluted child killer?

In the final verse Medea is urged not to carry out her plan to murder her children. Even at this stage the Chorus believe that Medea will not go through with this insane plan.

### The fourth *stasimon* (Lines 976-1001)

Again, this Choral Ode comprises of four verses, but again, there is no *epode*. The theme of this Choral Ode is primarily pity. The Chorus pity the children and the Princess Glauce in the first verse. In the second verse continues the lament for Glauce; for she is doomed.

The third verse is a verse that pities the fate of Jason; he will be widowed and childless by the end of the day. The final verse is a verse that pities Medea – she will lose her children through her own actions and has also been rejected by her husband.

### The fifth *stasimon* (Lines 1082-1117)

The fifth stasimon has four verses and an epode. The children have returned from their mission and now Medea has debated with herself whether to kill them or to spare their lives. She has decided to kill them in the previous episode and now awaits news of the fate of Glauce.

The theme of this Choral Ode is children in society. The Chorus outline an argument that women and men alike would be better if they remained childless.

Parents of children are, according to the Chorus, always afraid that their children will die, or that they have sufficient resources to raise children. The childless do not have these problems.

The Chorus conclude that children are an unwelcome gift of the Gods.

### The sixth *stasimon* (Lines 1252-1293)

The final stasimon has a different and innovative composition. It consists of verses and an epode, but is interrupted by the offstage cries of the children being murdered.

The Chorus begin this Ode by praying to Helios to stop Medea from carrying out her murder of the children. The Chorus then break off their singing whilst they hesitate over whether to intervene in saving the children.

They cannot intervene themselves. Traditionally the Tragic Chorus cannot intervene in the action on or off-stage, but instead act as observers.

The Chorus then seek a parallel for Medea – they sing of Ino, who also murdered her children.

**The end of the play**

The final words of the play are given to the Chorus. They sing of the unexpected and surprising end of the play;

*"The Unexpected God makes possible".*

*Task: The Chorus*

*Write a response to the following questions;*

a) *Explore what the Athenian audience would find unusual and interesting in the performance of the Chorus in Mede.*

- *You should discuss the participation of the Chorus and the themes they address in the choral odes in Medea.*

b) *To what extent do you agree with the Chorus that the end of the play was unexpected?*

## 3.3: Pollution, death and burial in *Medea*

This section will help you to;

- *Understand the importance of Pollution in Greek society and Medea.*

- *Understand the importance of burial in Greek Society.*

### Pollution in Ancient Greece and in *Medea*

**Key term: Pollution**

*An act that pollutes or makes unclean such as homicide, sacrileae or disease.*

In order for any society to function with order there were rules about what is acceptable and what is not. In Ancient Greece certain events were considered to be polluting; that is to say 'unclean and dangerous'. These polluting events included homicide, sacrilege and also certain contagious diseases, but also included madness. Other polluting acts included incest, infanticide and parricide.

These polluting acts and the individuals associated with them were thought to be capable of bringing disaster to the polis. Therefore steps were taken to remove polluted individuals. As a result a common punishment for being polluted was to be exiled.

Medea through her acts in the play was a polluted individual. By murdering her children Medea was guilty of infanticide, whilst hr murder of Glauce and Creon made her guilty of homicide. Medea had earlier murdered her brother and so was already tainted with pollution for this parricide before the play commenced.

### Death and burial in Ancient Greece

The rites associated with burial were an important part of being part of the *polis* or city-state in Ancient Greece. An Athenian of the fifth century had to be able to refer to, and account for, the burial of their ancestors in their *deme* in order to be enrolled as a citizen. Upon reaching adulthood, male citizens were scrutinised by their community in order to assess their eligibility for citizenship. If an applicant could not provide evidence that their parents were Athenian citizens, then they could not become citizens in turn.

Athenian citizens killed in war were often provided with a state burial. Thucydides records a funeral oration allegedly performed by Pericles at the start of the Peloponnesian War. Those bodies that could be recovered were present at the ceremony, whilst those that could not be recovered (perhaps lost on the battlefield) were remembered by an empty coffin.

The burial rites depicted in Homer's *Odyssey*, depict how a burial might be undertaken and the importance of correct practice of these rites in Greek thought. For example Odysseus forget to bury Elpenor in Book Ten; he was reminded by Elpenor's ghost in Book Eleven, Odysseus and his men ensure that he receives a decent burial in Book Twelve

The situation in epic is not that different to the world of tragedy: the correct rites of burial are especially important in Ancient Greek communities and tragedy after all, were the plays were performed as part of a communal as well as a religious event.

In Ancient Greece it was customary to accord the dead the right of burial. After a battle the request the return of their slain through the use of a herald was very rarely refused and often the defilement or desecration of the dead bodies was regarded as particularly abhorrent.

**Key terms:**
**Parricide and**
**Infanticide**

*Parricide: The murder of a blood relative.*

*Infanticide: The murder of a child*

In 480BC, for example the Spartan King Leonidas was killed in battle at Thermopylae by the Persians. According to Herodotus, after the battle the Persian King Xerxes had Leonidas' body beheaded and crucified. This was thereafter held up as a prime example of the savagery of 'barbarians'.

For Medea to refuse Jason the right to bury his own children was a barbarous act that again demonstrates the reversal of roles. Medea will bury the children, but the husband, Jason is denied any role in their burial and even to go to their graves.

## 3.4 Extension questions

### a) The Chorus

1) Consider each Choral song in Medea (including the parados) explore the subject matter they address and consider the relevance of this material to the play as a whole.

2) Explore what the Athenian audience would find unusual and interesting in the performance of the Chorus in Medea?

- You should discuss the participation of the Chorus and the themes they address in the choral odes in Medea.

3) How important to the plot is the role of the Choral leader in Medea?

### b) Jason

1) Who is responsible for Jason's downfall? Himself or Medea?

2) How far do you agree with the view that the play 'Medea' should in fact be called 'Jason'?

## 3.5 Glossary

*Acropolis:* The citadel of Athens where the Parthenon was built. Below and to the south-east is the site of the Theatre of Dionysus; to the south-west the Odeon of Herodes Atticus.

*Agon:* A competition, contest or trial.

*Agones* Competitions.

*Agonothetes:* A Festival and Games organizer or judge.

*Agora:* The marketplace area of Athens, to the north-east of the Acropolis, where the first performances of tragedy were staged.

*Amphidromia:* A ceremony that recognises a new born baby.

*Anagnorisis:* 'Recognition', as an aspect of play construction.

*Anapiesma:* A stage trap.

*Antistrophe:* The circular, turning dance-movement in a choral sequence, balancing and complementing a *strophe*.

*Archon:* One of a number of officials with responsibility for organizing Festivals.

*Auletes:* An *aulos*-player.

*Aulos:* The double-pipe used to accompany dramatic and dance performance.

*Barbaros:* A non-Greek, barbarian.

*Boule:* The Athenian Council.

*Choregia:* The office of being a *chorˆegos*.

*Choregos:* Private financier of part of an Athenian festival, or other state *leitourgia*. The word is also used for the leader of the Chorus: sometimes found in a choral ode as *choragos*

*Chorodidaskalos:* Choreographer.

*Choros:* Dance; hence the word became used for the Chorus in dramatic performance.

*Demos:* The Athenian people.

*Dithyrambos:* Dithyramb. A competitive dance for fifty performers from which, Aristotle believed, tragedy was derived.

*Ekklesia:* The Athenian Assembly which all male citizens were entitled to attend, with voting rights.

*Ekkuklema:* The wheeled platform which could be rolled out from backstage for *tableaux* or reveals.

*Eleos:* Pity (Aristotle).

*Episkenion:* The upper storey of the *skene.*

*Epodos:* Part of a lyric ode sung in a chorus following *strophe* and *antistrophe.*

*Erinyes:* 'Furies' Spirits of Gods of retribution for those who have committed a polluting crime – especially murder or parricide. According to Aeschylus the Erinyes were the daughters of Night and had snakes for hair.

*Exarchos:* Leader of a chorus.

*Exile:* A punishment in Ancient Greek Society often given for homicide, but also to rid a city of a polluted individual.

*Exodos:* The conclusion of a tragedy.

*Hamartia:* A fatal flaw in character.

*Hetaira: A* Courtesan or prostitute.

*Hubris:* The act of getting above oneself; wanton violence; insolence.

*Infanticide:* The murder of a child.

*Katharsis:* A purging or cleansing (medical term used by Aristotle for the emotional impact of tragedy).

*Kithara:* Lyre.

*Kommos:* A formal lament in tragedy, sometimes involving more than one character as well as the Chorus.

*Koruphaios:* Leader of the Chorus.

*Leitourgia:* A public service required of wealthy private citizens in Athens which might include meeting the expenses of dithyrambic or theatrical performance.

*Lyra:* A stringed instrument with a sounding-board made from a tortoise-shell.

*Mechane:* The stage crane which was raised to show characters, usually gods, in mid-air.

*Mechanopoios:* The operator of the *mechané*, probably located in one of the *parodoi.*

*Metics*, were resident foreigners. They take their name from the Greek word *'metoikos'* which means *'home changers'.*

*Mimesis:* A representation, impersonation or imitation.

*Odeion:* A roofed hall in the eastern side of the *theatron* in the Theatre of Dionysus in Athens.

*Orchestra:* The 'dancing-place' in a Greek theatre, between the stage and the auditorium, used in later times for the seats of dignitaries.

*Paraskenia:* The projecting side-structures in theatres which 'bounded' the performance space.

*Parodos:* The side-passage giving entry to the acting area from the sides; the first entry of a Chorus, usually, though not always, made along a side-passage.

*Parricide:* The murder of a family relative

*Peripeteia:* 'Reversal of expectation' in play construction

*Phobos:* Fear (Aristotle).

*Phorminx:* A type of lyre.

*Phyle:* A tribe or clan, one of the ten in Athens.

*Polis:* The 'city' or 'city-state'.

*Pollution:* An act that pollutes or makes unclean such as homicide, sacrilege or disease.

*Proagon* A preliminary to the dramatic festivals, held in the *Odeion*, when the competing playwrights presented their actors and the subject of their group of four plays.

*Proedria:* Stone seating in the *theatron*.

*Proskenion* The acting-area in front of the *skene*.

*Prosopon (prosopeion):* The face (the word used for 'mask').

*Protagonist:* The leading actor.

*Satyroi:* Satyrs, animalistic supporters of Dionysus. Each group of tragedies at the City Dionysia concluded with a satyr play (named after the chorus of satyrs).

*Skene:* With a literal meaning of 'tent', *skene* became the word used for the scenic facade from which actors entered and against which they played.

*Stasimon:* A choral song.

*Stegos:* Stage roof.

*Stichomythia:* Line-by-line balanced dialogue.

*Strophe* and *antistrophe:* The circular and complementary turning dance-movements in a choral sequence.

*Theatron:* The 'seeing-place'. The auditorium for spectators.

*Tragodos:* A writer of tragedies; a player in tragedies; the Chorus in tragedy.

*Tyrant:* An absolute ruler by other than right of succession.

## 3.6 Approximate dates of Euripides' plays

The dates of no more than a small number of plays are known with any certainty, either from the fragmentary surviving records or from other sources. Below is a reasonable chronological order for the plays written by Euripides.

The titles are given in an English version (often one of several) with the original transliterated from Greek or Latin in brackets.

Euripides lived between the years 485/4BC until 406 BC and wrote about ninety plays, of which nineteen survive, plus the only complete satyr play.

- **Alcestis** (*Alkestis*), 438
- **Medea** (*Medeia*), 431
- **Children of Heracles** (*Herakleidai*), *c.*430
- **Hippolytus** (*Hippolutos*), 428
- **Andromache** (*Andromache*), *c.*425
- **Electra** (*Elektra*), 425–413
- **Hecuba** (*Hekabe*), *c.*424
- **Cyclops** (*Kuklops*) (Satyr Play)
- **Suppliants** (*Hiketides*), 424–420
- **Trojan Women** (*Troiades*), 415
- **Heracles** (*Herakles*), *c.*415
- **Iphigenia among the Taurians** (*Iphigeneia he en Taurois*), *c.*414
- **Ion** (*Ion*), *c.*413
- **Helen** (*Helene*), 412
- **Phoenician Women** (*Phoinissai*), *c.*409
- **Orestes** (*Orestes*), 408
- **Iphigenia at Aulis** (*Iphigeneia he en Aulidi*), Performed posthumously in 405
- **Bacchae** (*Bakchai*), performed posthumously in 405
- **Rhesus** (*Rhesos*), believed by some not to be by Euripides

## 3.7 Further Reading

Besides reading this study guide and the tragedies thoroughly, you may wish to read further about Greek tragedy and the tragedians.

Baldock, M. *Greek Tragedy: an Introduction* 1989, Bristol Classical Press. ISBN 1853991198

Belgian School at Athens (2007) *Thorikos*, online [http://www.ebsa.info/Thorikos1.html]

Cartledge, P. 'The Greek Religious Festivals' in Easterling, P. E. and Muir, J. V. (eds). *Greek Religion and Society* 1985, Cambridge University Press. ISBN 0521287855

Cartledge, P. (2002) *The Greeks: A Portrait of Self and Others,* Oxford University Press

Csapo, E. and Slater, W.J. (1994) *The Context of Ancient Drama*, University of Michigan

Crane, G. *Perseus 2.0* (PIP) 2000, Yale University Press www.yalebooks.co.uk

Cropp, M. J. *Euripides: 'Electra'* 1988, Aris & Phillips. ISBN 085668239X

Dugdale, E. (2008) *Greek Theatre in Context,* Cambridge University Press

Easterling, P. E. *The Cambridge Companion to Greek Tragedy* 1997, Cambridge University Press. ISBN 0521412455

Garland, R. *Religion and the Greeks* 1994, Bristol Classical Press. ISBN 185399409X

Goldhill, S. *Reading Greek Tragedy* 1986, Cambridge University Press. ISBN 0521315794

Green, P. (1996) *The Greco-Persian Wars*, University of California Press

Hall, E. (1989) *Inventing the barbarian: Greek Self Definition through Tragedy,* Oxford University Press

Harrison, T. (ed) (2001) *Greeks and Barbarians (Edinburgh Readings on the Ancient World),* Edinburgh University Press

Hogan, J. C. *A Commentary on the Complete Greek Tragedies: Aeschylus* 1985, University of Chicago Press. ISBN 0226348431
JACT, *The World of Athens* 1984, Cambridge University Press. ISBN 0521273897

Morgan, J. *Hellenika Photo CD* 2004, J-PROGS www.j-progs.com

Morgan, J. OCR AS Classical Civilisation OxBox CD-ROM (2008) ISBN: 9780199126606

Morgan, J. OCR A2 Classical Civilisation OxBox CD-ROM (2009) ISBN: 9780199126613

Storey, I. C. and Allan, A. (2013) *A Guide to Ancient Greek Drama (Blackwell Guides to Classical Literature)*, John Wiley & Sons

Taplin, O. *Greek Tragedy in Action* 2002, Routledge. ISBN 041530251X

Taylor, D. W. *The Greek and Roman Stage* 1999, Bristol Classical Press. ISBN 1853995916

Wiesehöfer, J. (2006) *Ancient Persia from 550 BC to 650 AD,* I.B. Tauris Arnott, P. D. *An Introduction to the Greek Theatre* 1965, Macmillan. ISBN 0333079132

Wiles, D. (2000) *Greek Theatre Performance: An Introduction,* Cambridge University Press

Printed in Great Britain
by Amazon